THE GIRL WITH THE WIDOW'S PEAK

The Memoirs

THE GIRL WITH THE WIDOW'S PEAK

The Memoirs

Lady Ursula d'Abo

Edited by
Professor David Watkin

Foreword by
John Julius Norwich

Published by d'Abo Publications
37 Buckingham Court, Kensington Park Road, London, W11 3BP

Designed in Chipping Campden by Loose Chippings
The Paddocks, Chipping Campden, Gloucestershire, GL55 6AU
www.loosechippings.org

Printed and bound in England by The Dorset Press,
Dorchester, DT1 1HD

Hardback ISBN 978-1-907991-09-7
eBook ISBN 978-1-907991-10-3

Contents

The author is very grateful to the following for their valued support in publishing this book:
Rosemary Andreae, Gergely Battha-Pajor, Paul Doyle, James and Mary Miller, John Martin Robinson, David Watkin and Jocelyne Wilson

Foreword

Lady Ursula d'Abo
An appreciation by her cousin, Viscount Norwich

After my parents and my Nanny, Ursula was the first person I ever remember. Most children's earliest memories are of Christmas, and Christmas for me as a child was always Belvoir. Belvoir Christmases were memorable indeed, with the whole family – all the sisters and the cousins and the aunts – bringing with them their attendant valets, ladies' maids, nannies, governesses, even tutors. How many extra mouths did my uncle John have to feed for the last ten days of every year? I dread to think.

Of the children's generation – my cousins, there must have been nearly twenty of us – Ursula was the oldest, I the youngest, she was thirteen years older than me, already a grown-up when I first remember her. But she was different from the others. She was extremely funny, for one thing; I remember my Nanny saying, 'Oh, that Lady Ursula, she's a real character, she is.' And – heaven knows why – she seemed to take a genuine interest in me. As I grew a bit older, she began to read me stories; when I was perhaps eight or nine, we sang songs together at the piano. By then I could vamp accompaniments to most songs, but did she or I do the playing? Alas, I can't remember.

What I do remember, very clearly indeed, is how superb she looked on a horse. I can see her now at the Belvoir meet: side-saddle, black skirt to the ankle, netted hair under top hat. Hunting has never had much of a message for me in my adulthood, but then – oh how I longed to be riding off with that dazzling company.

Looking back now, when time has narrowed the age gap between us – in fact, I suspect that Ursula feels a good deal younger than I do – my one regret is that we have not seen each other in our later lives anything like as often as I would have liked. But the great figures of one's childhood remain close for ever – and Cousin Ursula is perhaps the greatest.

John Julius Norwich
19 February 2014

Editor's Preface

Born in November 1916 as the first-born child of the Marquess of Granby who was to succeed his father as 9th Duke of Rutland in 1925, Lady Ursula is a sprightly and still glamorous lady whose memoirs of her highly unusual life make riveting reading. Life at Belvoir Castle, Leicestershire, where she was brought up, was maintained on a feudal scale until September 1939. We are thus fortunate that, describing herself as having been an observant child, Lady Ursula is able to bring this to life with her vivid accounts including those of the numerous servants and their roles from liveried footmen to the pig man.

She also describes her close relationship with her father whose favourite child she was. Even at the age of eight, she helped him in his sensitive restoration of another Manners family seat, the mediaeval Haddon Hall, Derbyshire, which had become ruinous. Clever and sophisticated, a perfectionist in all things, her father was a passionate antiquarian, collector, and lover of beauty. He was a tremendous influence on Ursula who was heartbroken when he died, tragically young, aged fifty-three, in 1940. In 1916, as Lord Granby, he had married Kathleen Tennant who had left for Westminster Abbey from No. 10 Downing Street, where her uncle, Herbert Asquith, later 1st Earl of Oxford and Asquith, was prime minister and married to the lively

Margot Tennant. Lord Granby left from the grandiose Rutland town house at 16 Arlington Street.

Lady Ursula describes her coming-out Ball at Belvoir Castle in 1934 at the age of seventeen and also how in the same year she was seduced at Belton House by the fifty-year-old Lord Brownlow. He became Lord in Waiting to King Edward VIII whom she met with Mrs Simpson in the south of France after the abdication. In common with her whole family, she played a role in the Coronation of King George VI and Queen Elizabeth in 1937. Dressed by Norman Hartnell, she was one of the Six Maids of Honour who bore the Queen's train in Westminster Abbey. She appeared in photographs on the balcony of Buckingham Palace next to Queen Elizabeth, and Princesses Elizabeth and Margaret. In 1938 she accompanied the new King and Queen on their triumphant first state visit to Paris and Versailles in 1938.

By contrast, her war work was soon to include being in charge of hundreds of women at a munitions factory in Springfield, Grantham. Her activities here were described in letters, quoted in this book, which her glamorous aunt, Lady Diana Cooper, wife of Duff Cooper, 1st Viscount Norwich, wrote to their son John Julius while a schoolboy.

Though her father had expected her to follow family custom by marrying into the peerage, ideally a Duke or his heir, she chose as her husband Anthony

Marreco, a barrister, whom she married in 1943 in the chapel at Belvoir Castle, wearing a dress by Worth of Paris. The marriage was unsuccessful and she travelled to India at the invitation of the Maharajah of Jaipur. She became a friend of Nehru and recalls a life of feudal grandeur in the Pink Palace at Jaipur on a scale even more lavish than that she had known at Belvoir, including Tiger shoots, polo matches, and Hindu festivals.

Later she was courted by two young men, Johnnie Montagu-Douglas-Scott, Earl of Dalkeith and future Duke of Buccleuch, and Erland d'Abo whom she married in 1951. He died in 1970 and she had an affair with Paul Getty which is described in this book. Her memoirs include accounts of her life at West Wratting Park, Cambridgeshire, where she brought up her three children whose lives are also recorded. The text is about 40,000 words long and the illustrations include unpublished drawings by Rex Whistler, a close friend who greatly admired her, as well as a photograph of her by Cecil Beaton, and one of her with the Royal Family on the balcony of Buckingham Palace at the Coronation of 1937. The story told is unforgettable, and though it has touches of Brideshead and Downton Abbey, it is utterly novel for, unlike them, it is actually real.

Professor David Watkin
Cambridge, 22 November 2013

To my darling children: Henry, Louisa and Dick

Chapter One
Sitting In Silver

Here am I. A little girl in my best frock, not with a silver spoon but sitting in a huge Charles II silver wine cooler, just big enough for my sister and me. I am a child about five years old, embarking on life. Unable then to know where the 20th century would blow me: here, there and everywhere.

My life has spanned most of an extraordinary century. I was born on the 8th November 1916. My very early childhood was spent most of the time with my Nanny and my old grandfather at Belvoir Castle on top of a hill overlooking trees. It was a Victorian world. My grandfather, who seemed even older than the castle, was Henry John Brinsley Manners, 8th Duke of Rutland, but I called him Appa and was totally spoilt by him. He was eighty-six years old and had a nurse called Sister Malone who was as big as him and wore a starched white cap from ear to ear.

Everyone in the castle loved her and so did I. She used to walk my grandfather in a wheelchair to the Duke's Walk in the park and back again and I would always follow, trotting along by his side. We would sit for a while in the summer house which was made of moss and wooden boughs and had a thatched roof.

The view below embraced spreading gardens and gravel walks and a huge wood leading to the main drive. The gardens were beautifully kept with terraces of flowers and shrubs and specimen trees and – it has always stuck in the memory – an extraordinary monkey puzzle tree. I loved the scented azaleas and the rhododendrons, under which convenient benches nestled at the top of stone steps flanked with stone urns. It was a truly romantic English garden. On the other side of the summer house, a walk of over two miles led towards Frog Hollow, a little lake with springs of water at different levels enclosed by mown grassy swards where grazed life-size lead statues of deer, placed there by my grandmother, an artist. They enhanced the illusion of civilisation created on the 'wild side of the forest'.

Overlooking that was another folly called the Devil's Knocker, with a huge front door and an enormous knocker on it, set in a sort of grotto. A third folly had stained glass windows and was set in the same sort of recessed grotto. All this vast domain required maintenance on a scale unimaginable today, with teams of gardeners and woodsmen constantly working. As I grew up I realised just how beautifully it was kept, under the watchful eye of my grandfather, a conscientious and public-spirited landowner who had devoted his life to Belvoir.

The castle was my playground and my fiefdom. There was a kitchen with at least twenty people bustling around, and a still-room packed with all sorts of delicious jams, preserves and pickles. Fresh bread was made every day and put out to rise in front of the stove. The smell was irresistible and I very naughtily used to put my fingers in and twiddle round the warm dough, only to be ticked off and chased back laughing and screaming to the nursery. I knew my grandfather adored me and I could do no wrong in his castle.

I was very observant and there was nothing I didn't know about what went on below stairs, because the nursery corridor was adjacent to the chapel and the kitchen below. I used to see all sorts of glorious things. Rows of silver dishes with soufflés rising a mile high. Great big copper cauldrons permanently simmering on the stove making stock from all the food scraps. Everything went into them to be clarified, including egg shells, and there was a clever little tap at the bottom which you would turn to release the most aromatic juices. There was a huge quantity of copper saucepans always being cleaned by the cheeky young boys in the kitchen. They didn't want to stand in puddles so they would lay out wooden duck-boards in rows on the flagstones with various cloths for mopping up. I loved to dash in and tease them by throwing the damp cloths and would turn and run away before they could retaliate.

In those days it was almost feudal. All the departments in the castle had their own heads of department. The housekeeper Mrs Forbes held the most exalted position and had her own room where only the butlers, head footmen and visiting ladies' maids would eat. She used to rustle bombastically around the castle looking after all the staff and visitors. Mrs Forbes had been head housemaid in other great houses and when she was promoted became my mother's right hand. She was immensely capable and took charge of arranging everything so Mother barely lifted a finger.

Our indomitable cook Mrs Anderson was from Troon in Scotland. She had started working in a famous house as a kitchen maid at the age of fourteen and came to us as an experienced cook. She used to read tea leaves, and instead of learning to cook, my girlfriends and I would rush to the kitchen to get our fortunes told. There was nothing she couldn't do. At Christmas one year she cooked a boar's head with the most delicious stuffing and with the face of the boar a galantine, with the tusks remaining white. It tasted as good as it looked and we ate every single mouthful.

The castle was entirely self-supporting. Flowers, vegetables and fruit came from our own gardens and orchards, and hams from dear old Mr Chettle, the pig man, resplendent in whiskers and huge baggy trousers. He made a beer vat into a huge cauldron for pigswill to which was added all the kitchen leftovers at the castle, which we children were allowed to stir. As we pulled up the sluice gate the swill flowed into a wooden trough he had made and the roar of the piglets was never to be forgotten. We children were absolutely thrilled by this. He would fatten the pigs, cure them and turn them into delicious hams. Some of the pigs were sold and he would weigh the head and charge his customers by that, but most of the hams went off to the castle. He also looked after the poultry. Our eyes were on sticks when he placed the hens on a tripod, inserted a catheter into their behinds and pedalled away like on a sewing machine to force feed them. When they were nice and fat, he would pluck them, truss them in a proper way with a bow on the side until they were perfectly ready for cooking and lay them out on enormous trays. Then an odd-job man would come and carry them up to the castle on his head.

Mr Gibson the gardener never went to the Great War because he was already too old. The former

Duchess, wife of the 5th Duke two centuries earlier, had come from Castle Howard and when she saw the gardens were two miles from the house she created the pleasure grounds adjoining the castle at vast expense, moving hills and tons of soil. She planted azaleas and a marvellous selection of rare Himalayan rhododendrons which Mr Gibson propagated with great skill. He was particularly gifted when it came to greenery and grew one cymbidium orchid with no less than thirty two blooms on each spike. Mother liked to have the same flowers in huge tanks in the banqueting hall at Haddon and he grew all species of delphiniums especially. He was brilliant at the propagation of plants. When my sister came back from her honeymoon in the Pacific she brought back hundreds of snippets and he had the whole lot in flower by the following year. He was normally sweet and placid but could turn into a savage beast when the war-evacuee children from London tried to steal his rhubarb sticks and hid them in their shorts, but he could always see the stems poking out.

Appa absolutely adored me and used to creep into my bedroom and give me delicious pink sweets saying: 'Shhh, don't make a noise or Nanny will find out'. My parents, predominantly my mother, were very social and lived a lot everywhere, visiting friends, travelling and entertaining, and I was regularly dumped with dear old Nanny. She looked like a Chinese lady, with small eyes and long black plaits and I adored her. In those days Nanny mattered, nursery mattered and one only went to the drawing room on special occasions for tea. Dressed in our finery, which consisted of dresses in starched white cotton and big red sashes with bows and matching little red shoes, we entered with some trepidation and very much on our best behaviour.

My father John was Appa's second son and although his elder brother had died he hadn't yet inherited, and so we lived between a small farmhouse in Derbyshire called the Wood House and London. I was king pin until my younger sister Isabel arrived. We couldn't have been more different in personality: I was shy and sensitive whereas she was loud and gregarious. My father always said it was because she was born in a Zeppelin raid and had been trying to make herself heard ever since. She would not stop talking at night until eventually my father made a hole in the wall of the bedroom above her bed so Nanny could cope with the situation and say: 'Get back to sleep, Isabel'.

My brother Charles followed soon after and we three were so close in age we were like triplets. My nose was thoroughly put out of joint when my brother arrived, as my parents passionately wanted an heir, and even Nanny was obsessed about it. After two daughters the birth of a son was greeted with universal rapture, and everything from then on seemed to centre around the new baby and heir. I remember being bored and playing endlessly with guinea pigs in the garden. I gave one a foxglove as a special treat and the poor thing died the next day, poisoned by the digitalis.

I had pale skin and ink black hair with a widow's peak and was constantly asking questions. As children we were dressed in very ordinary, washable, straight linen dresses, except when we went to tea in the drawing room when we would change into frocks with silk sashes and white frillies. When young I used to sew very well and also loved to ride. My father loathed hunting although we had the famous Belvoir hunt in the grounds, but I virtually lived on a horse as a child and used to ride my pony everywhere. We kept the ponies in the most wonderful Charles II stables at Belvoir. I was a daredevil on horseback and went like smoke. When we hunted, the Master of Hounds was terrified we would get squashed in the gates, and with his whip would hold up the two hundred horses behind us so Isabel and I could go safely through first. The Belvoir hunt was spectacular. Sometimes in the 1920s and 30s the Prince of Wales, later Edward VIII, would join us and we would gallop for twelve miles from Belvoir to Melton Mowbray entirely on grass, with no plough and no wire fences, just neat hedges. The only obstacle was the River Smite which one could jump in certain places. Other horses waded through or swam, depending on where the foxes went.

My grandmother Violet, Duchess of Rutland, nicknamed Noona, wasn't there very often. She lived largely in London where she was a great social hostess as well as a well-known artist whom Rodin admired. She had studied in Paris and produced hundreds of portrait drawings, now all over the world.

When her eldest son was only nine years old he twisted a gut from turning a somersault and died tragically. (Of course nowadays he probably could have been operated on and saved). She had been besotted with him and was demented with grief. In an almost hypnotic state she was persuaded to sculpt a life-size recumbent figure of him which was much admired. I remember my father telling me he had sat for the feet. The original is in the Tate Gallery in London. For years the cast was rolled up in straw under the staircase at Belvoir in a wooden crate. Only when I became older did she make a plinth on which to place the recumbent figure with medallions of herself and her husband at either end of the figure, and her sisters-in-law, the Marchioness of Anglesey, Lady Violet Benson, and Lady Diana Cooper, on the sides. The plinth was well carved but did not have the same intensity and flair as the figure. She was elderly by the time she completed the work.

A Lindsay of Balcarres, she came from one of the most cultivated and artistic families, noted as patrons, collectors and bibliophiles. She herself was a completely professional artist and was constantly drawing as she talked. She also played the piano well and dressed very originally, never losing her lovely auburn hair, which in her old age she wore in a lace cap, sitting up in bed. Beauty was her theme and she simply couldn't have anything around her that wasn't pretty or original. She redecorated all the family rooms at Belvoir, buying pretty things to enhance them. Her enthusiasm rubbed off on my father, John.

I used to visit my grandmother when she was living in London, off Buckingham Palace Road. There Noona had two rooms joined together and made into one marvellous library with French doors opening onto the garden. Rex Whistler was her great friend and helped her with the design of this room. Rex was born at Eltham, Kent in 1905 and studied at the Slade School of Art. Aged twenty-two, he completed his first big commission: a huge mural in the restaurant of the Tate Gallery, London – soon to be dubbed 'the most amusing room in Europe'. Later he carried out other mural commissions, including those at Port Lympne, Kent, Mottisfont, Hampshire, and – his masterpiece – the forty-seven-foot Claudian fantasy at Plas Newydd, Isle of Anglesey. During his time at Plas Newydd he became the lover of my cousin

Lady Caroline Paget, daughter of my Aunt Marjorie, and painted numerous portraits of her, including a startling nude. He was perhaps best known for his exquisite book illustrations for *Gulliver's Travels* and Hans Andersen's *Fairy Tales* and for his fine theatre designs.

Before he was famous he came to stay at Haddon as Father had commissioned him to paint the summer house at Haddon as viewed from the hills opposite. This work is still there, hanging over the mantelpiece in the Long Gallery. We became great friends and he was quite keen on me. When I was at school in Italy he used to send me such amusing letters with wonderful drawings. Even the envelopes would be covered with pictures – sometimes the stamp would appear as the centre of a red watering can. He would also send us the most amusing rebus puzzle letters where he drew pictures to replace words.

I remember one of my brothers being home from school, ill and miserable in bed. Rex used to go and entertain him by drawing every kind of monster which, when you rotated it, would turn into a man. He was such an attractive man with an original sense of humour and could do anything with a pen and paper. At the outbreak of war he took a commission in the Welsh Guards Armoured Division. Everyone tried to persuade him that his talents would be better served at home but he was adamant. He painted the inside of his tank to give distance as he was quite claustrophobic. Shortly after embarking for Normandy in July 1944, he was killed by a mortar shell on his first day in action. He was thirty-nine.

Noona used to ask me to lunch frequently, which was inevitably roast chicken cooked by her limping old maid Felgate, and quiz me about the latest gossip amongst the young people. She had lived originally in a charming eighteenth century house, designed by James Gibbs and given to her by the Duke of Portland, at the bottom end of Arlington Street facing St James's Park.

My parents' wedding took place at Westminster Abbey in January 1916 and my father was married from the house in Arlington Street while my mother got married from 10 Downing Street, where her uncle, Herbert Asquith, was Prime Minister. Asquith's wife Margot was a Tennant and entered society together with her sister Laura in 1881. They became the central female figures of the aristocratic group of intellectuals known as 'The Souls'. When she married Herbert Asquith, she brought him into the glittering social world he had not experienced with his first wife. She also became the unwilling stepmother of his five children, including his eldest daughter Violet who married Maurice Bonham Carter. Violet is the grandmother of the lovely actress Helena Bonham

Carter. Margot was an accomplished writer and known for her acerbic wit. A possibly apocryphal story related her meeting with the movie star Jean Harlow and correcting her mispronunciation of her first name, saying 'No, no: the 't' is silent, as in 'Harlow'.

My favourite story about my parents' wedding relates to father's eldest sister, Lady Victoria Manners, who was always known by her second name Marjorie. She had married Charles Paget, 6th Marquess of Anglesey, in 1912 but it was a rather tumultuous relationship. He stormed out after one year for no known reason and was gone for months. Later the gossip was that he sailed away on his yacht. Marjorie didn't hear or see anything more of him until he turned up on the morning of my parents' wedding as if nothing had happened, ringing the bell and asking whether Marjorie was dressed and ready to go. Father and Mother never knew until they came down the aisle and saw them sitting together in the front pew.

To the astonishment of my parents they remained happily together for ever after and had six beautiful children. After four daughters the longed-for heir arrived when finally twins were born, one of which was a boy, Henry, who became the 7th Marquess. After a distinguished military career in the Second World War Henry became famous as an author and military historian, writing a seven-volume history of the British cavalry and a marvellous book about his ancestor losing a leg at Waterloo, *One Leg: The Life and Letters of 1ˢᵗ Marquess of Anglesey*, which was published in 1961. The 1ˢᵗ Marquess who was on his horse next to Wellington said 'By God, I've lost my leg', and Wellington replied: 'By God. So you have'. His blood-spattered uniform trousers and wooden leg are still on display at Plas Newydd, the Anglesey home.

On the death of my grandfather in May 1925 my father inherited all the estates of the dukedom and we moved from Wood House. My mother Kathleen was from the famous Tennant family, great industrialists in Glasgow who had made their fortune out of bleach. Their factory had a huge chimney called the Tennant Stalk, one of the largest chimneys ever built and a major landmark in the Second City of Scotland. She was one of five children and was very, very beautiful, talented and gentle and universally adored. She acquired the nickname of Kakoo, which stuck with her all her life. Gardening was one of her favourite occupations and I can remember her at Haddon on a ladder lodged on one of the big buttresses. There she was, perilously perched, planting lots of tiny plants with bright colours on the grey buttresses. The rose garden there was her creation.

She also had an almost supernatural gift with animals which we all inherited; my sons and daughter too. She used to tame a bullfinch out of its nest, when she knew from its feathers that it was a cock, with an ink black head and a scarlet bosom (whereas the females were dowdy brown). She would feed it on mashed oatmeal on an orange stick, and this little bird would become her shadow and looked upon its cage as its home. She used to hold out the cage wherever she was and the bird would fly in. It would fly around her in the castle and even when she was outdoors, and then go to sleep in its dear little cage. One particular evening I remember dining with a smart party at the castle. The bullfinch was perched on a bracket near the fireplace and obviously enjoying the goings-on of this dinner party. When it came to dessert, which was served on beautiful Dr Wall Worcester porcelain plates with painted flowers and butterflies and gold knives and forks, Mother poured some water into her bowl and the bird flew down and had a bath, to general delight. When the men stayed on to drink port, Mother wouldn't even bother to call as she left and the bird would follow her out of the room, singing away in her wake.

I was dumped quite often with my Tennant grandparents at their house at Lossiemouth in Morayshire, now a famous golf course, where my grandparents' garden opened on to the ninth tee.

My old maternal grandfather loved playing golf and used to take me out of an afternoon at Hindford at North Berwick. He let me try all his clubs, which in those days were made of wood, not iron and gave me my own little putter. Later the Tennants took a house at Innes, near North Berwick, for the summer holidays and all their grandchildren came to stay. There would be one governess in charge of everyone and after lunch we were made to rest and read books. Afterwards, we were questioned on what we had read, and I have always loved reading and books. There were also expeditions and treats. Of all the seaside adventures we had there I enjoyed camping overnight. I don't remember parents being there but we always had two amusing girl cousins, Laura and Anne Charteris. Laura was not the prettiest, but great fun, while Anne was, even then, beautiful. Their mother Frances had died when the girls were young and they spent their holidays with Isabel and me at Belvoir. They were always with the party at Innes in August. They became well known when they grew up, as Laura married the Duke of Marlborough and Anne fell in love with Ian Fleming of James Bond fame, while still married to the newspaper magnate Lord Harmsworth. In the end she ran off and lived in Jamaica with Ian.

Another ritual of our summer holidays was to stay with the Colquhouns at Ross-Dhu on the bonny banks of Loch Lomond. It was a pretty Georgian house with excellent pictures and library, and a sort of colonnaded entrance hall reached by steps. My mother's sister Aunt Dinah and her husband Ian, chief of the Colquhoun clan, were both immense 'characters'. Our cousins were our age and we boated about the loch and were a permanent nuisance, I fear. Aunt Dinah, a typical Scot, was a frugal hostess and used to feed us on tough local fish called powan straight from the loch. It was always powan, powan, powan. Uncle Ian walked bare-foot round the breakfast table playing the bagpipes dressed in kilt and sporran and we had to follow him in procession. He went everywhere bare-footed, even Spitzbergen. The horror of being made to sit and eat salty porridge out a wooden bowl was outweighed by the gorgeousness of the berries from their walled garden – raspberries, blackcurrants and Japanese wineberries all cultivated in their greenhouse, as was the fashion in that part of Scotland.

I was always my father's favourite as well as his eldest. He took me everywhere and involved me in all his interest and activities. Dukes in those days were thrown into everything happening in the locality, whether in a position of authority or not, and he was involved in the affairs of Lincolnshire, Leicestershire and Derbyshire. As a tiny girl he took me to the Rolls Royce firm in Derby where they were testing a Rolls

Royce engine to go into the first airplane. It was in a corrugated shed which would have fallen down if the whole thing exploded. When it started the noise was something unparalleled. It did not bring the shed crashing down and everyone was thrilled by the success of the test.

Another time Father took me to a speed test of the Flying Scotsman which was to take place on a special test rail that the railway company had built at Grantham, our local town. There were two coaches at the back of the Flying Scotsman engine. No 'health and safety' then. Father and I got on board the flying plate in the engine: the chief engineer, his mate stoking the coal and little me. We were so squashed I had to move to one side each time he raised his shovel to stoke the engine. I was even allowed to pull the whistle and was overwhelmed by the roar as we sped off. There was nothing that could give you the sensation of speed, and wobble, better than being on a steam engine of that size. When I grew up I used to love watching this train speeding through Grantham station on a frosty night with sparks flying in the sky. It was a breath-taking sight, and I had – almost – driven one!

Haddon Hall, the Derbyshire home of the Rutlands, dates from 1066 and was built over many centuries, being completed around 1553 during the time of Queen Elizabeth. The heiress Dorothy

Vernon had eloped with John Manners in 1558, and it had been a favourite house in the 16th century. But it was then left empty for over one hundred years. My grandfather loved the place and used to go there to fish, but would stay at the Peacock Hotel, as the Hall was almost a ruin. Apart from keeping the rain out he would never restore it. It was my father's boyhood dream to do so and he started collecting oak furniture to fill it when he was still at Eton, buying discarded pieces from local cottages and farms.

When grandfather died, father immediately started work on reviving Haddon, spending every spare penny he had, and making this his life's great achievement. The Wood House, where we lived as children, was a little north of Rowsley Village and from there Nanny used to drive us in a tub cart pulled by a pony for picnics to Haddon whilst it was being restored. The motor car was still a new invention. My father had a Renault which mainly sat in the garage as a very valuable possession. He loved that car with a passion and used to clean and polish it for hours, even down to the brass exhaust pipes. There were three passenger seats and no windows; it was open to the wind. My sister and I used to sit on the floor with our feet dangling out either side, trying to work the enormous rubber horn.

My father was his own architect at Haddon and along with the wonderful Clerk of the Works, Mr

Stanhope, supervised even the really difficult things like underpinning one of the collapsing towers and putting a new roof on the banqueting hall, which he did with beams of oak weathered in the engine room at Belvoir. Mr Stanhope loved the building as much as Father did and, because the house hadn't been changed or spoiled in the Victorian era, they were able to restore it as a perfect example of a medieval house and garden. Father had some specialist advice from Noona's brother, Major Lindsay, who was one of the 'Souls' (arty, cultivated Edwardians who loved beautiful things), and who helped his various relations restore old houses – including Aunt Marjorie's husband's house at Beaudesert, Staffordshire, the historic seat of the Paget family, which was to be demolished in 1935. Harold Brakespear, an architect involved with work at St George's Chapel, Windsor, also provided historical designs for the Hall roof at Haddon. Uncle Lindsay's wife Nora was a famous garden designer and shared in Mother's replanting of the old gardens which surround the house.

Chapter Two
Governesses and Growing Up

As I grew up I graduated from the nursery to the school room. Governesses came and went, for unless Mother liked them they didn't have a chance. It was never a question of whether or not they could teach. One governess who really got me going and enthusiastic about lessons was sacked within four months, even though I adored her. She taught me total concentration and I learned a lot from her, especially mathematics. Sadly, after she left maths was never pursued. In due course Isabel joined me in the schoolroom and we would sit together for what seemed like hours with very straight backs at the end of the dining room table. But we had a general education steeped in the arts, and learned to create beautiful things by hand.

Isabel and I could be very naughty while learning because we were so boisterous and full of life. From the moment we woke up in the morning we wanted to do everything that was physical, not just sitting down and concentrating on French grammar. We were the greatest friends as children, and defended each other over punishments. Isabel was gregarious and a tomboy at heart, while I was quieter and more feminine. Conversation and flirtatiousness came naturally to Isabel. She was beautiful with large green eyes, pale skin and curly black hair. I must admit that, as I grew up, at moments I was a tiny bit jealous of her because she attracted men so easily.

When I was eight I was proud to help my father with the restoration at Haddon. We worked together on the mullion windows in the beautiful Long Gallery. The small panes were a diamond pattern of greenish glass. They caught the light as the panes were set wobbly, which nobody had ever seen before. The lead, mined locally in the 16th century, was full of silver. Father melted it down in a great beer vat and, at exactly the right temperature, poured it out onto a billiard table where the baize cloth had been removed to form flat sheets of lead. It was completely pliable in the heat and we would roll it up and pull it through a wooden mould into narrow strips. I used to sit on a block of stone in the top courtyard at Haddon watching him do this, utterly fascinated. When the glass was cleaned we used to run to put it back, and we would be given a spigot to flatten the lead panes for the glass. The other children were soon easily bored but I enjoyed it wildly, and it gives me extra pleasure when I walk up and down the gallery, to remember it all so vividly.

While restoring the chapel at Haddon I discovered some medieval frescoes which had been whitewashed over in the Reformation. Father had erected scaffolding and we were allowed to help pick the whitewash off. I was told to go with my knife to the highest bit at the far end as I was fearless. To my amazement a flake the size of my nail broke off, and then one the size of my hand to reveal a little ship with people in it. We worked on the wall opposite the entrance and uncovered a life-size painting of St Christopher crossing a stream with fish swimming in it. My father was very impressed and longed to restore the frescoes properly. He invited Professor Tristram, the great expert from London, to come down and advise. Unfortunately, although the Professor was perfectly charming, he used a sort of wash or glue to fix the murals which actually made the colours more faded than they had been before.

Father was a passionate antiquarian and collector. He excavated the ruins of Croxton Abbey on the estate at Belvoir and discovered the Norman tombs of the Todeni family, founders of the castle, which he placed in the private chapel there. (Lord

Roos, one of the Norman barons, has lead eyes in his stone effigy). He was a keen philatelist and had a special interest in coins and medals. He also collected medieval tiles. His tile collection is now in the British Museum. He collected eggs of rare birds and architectural items which were stored in a special museum room which also housed the archives at Belvoir.

His great achievement was to sort and catalogue the archives. In one of the towers was the Muniment Room, where there were hundreds of tin boxes containing deeds with beautiful original seals. He would set to and painstakingly mend the seals with a little lamp and sealing wax, which he heated and manipulated with dentists' tools to flatten them and replace missing parts. Some of the documents were difficult to read as they were old and faded and written in strange script. (I remember a charming letter from Charles II to his wife calling her 'My dear little whiffy-whoffy'). To solve this problem Father rigged up an infra-red lamp in the tower with two carbons, about a foot high and two inches in diameter. When you put them together with electricity it would make a tremendous flash of light. He was really taking infra-red photographs, a new technology for reading old documents. He was always ahead of his time and I was fascinated by him, as in his company something riveting would happen every day. He was an education in himself. My interests in history, homes and things came from him and the happy times when he patiently involved me in his work.

He got up at eight every morning, had breakfast at nine and then started work. He had three Labradors he loved, called Quest, Polar and Belvoir. They were pale coloured and so beautifully trained that when he went out fly fishing at Haddon he would never take a net. The first dog would swim in to collect the fish and then drop it at father's feet and you would never know it had been touched. The other two would wait patiently, trembling with anticipation until it was their turn. Father would also use binoculars to find plovers' nests, point in that direction and the dogs would go off one by one and bring back the eggs unbroken, their mouths were so soft.

He was equally demanding with his children. We had always to be neat, tidy, clean and properly behaved, but there was a lot of fun too. We ate formally, always three courses and white linen. The Chelsea porcelain dessert plates in the dining room were beautiful, and were washed by hand by the housekeeper. We were brought up from the beginning to respect lovely things. We got dressed beautifully for dinner every night and an old boy that used to bring the coals in – no small job in such a large place – would ring a dressing gong at eight o'clock, half an hour before dinner, and then another at half past eight to indicate everything was ready to be served.

Every year at Christmas there was a Servants' Ball. Father would dance with the housekeeper, Mother with the chef and Isabel and I with the first and second footmen. They would be attired in their full dress livery with white ties, while my sister and I wore seasonally appropriate red velvet. An enormous Christmas tree was erected in the hall and gifts distributed to the village children. One year we had real oranges and lemons which were so rare we gave the servants one each.

We used to go to London for periods where I was taught to swim at the Bathing Club and went to dancing classes. I had seen the ballet many times and passionately wanted to go on the stage. Eventually I had lessons with the great Russian ballerina Tamara Karsavina. Despite her triumphs with Diaghilev in St Petersburg and Paris she now had to teach because she had escaped from the Revolution with not a penny to her name. She was a great martinet but highly educated and amusing. Her memoir *Theatre Street* is superb. Apparently she thought I had a great aptitude but I was not allowed to pursue it. She finally married the British diplomat, Henry James Bruce. No frills on her. During the class she would beat time on the upright piano with a violin wand, I think to the horror of the pianist, which she would aim at our feet if they weren't turned out properly. She was not a beauty and when teaching looked like a Red Indian squaw with her face covered with cold cream. She would suddenly announce the class was over as she was going to lunch, and then emerge looking like the Firebird to go to the Ritz with some glamorous type.

I was also keen on the piano and was taught by various people either at home, in London or at the castle. I loved classical music and enjoyed playing Chopin preludes. My grandmother Noona, a perfectionist and professional artist, tried to teach me from the start. This consisted of making me play every kind of scale over and over again, which became slightly irksome, however beneficial. All the houses we lived in had grand pianos and I would play a lot on my own for pleasure. When I started going to balls I very much took to Cole Porter and collected a book of his songs which I played just for fun. I felt passionately about his lyrics which resonated with my dawning romantic imaginings, especially my favourite:

> *Night and day you are the one*
> *Only you beneath the moon or under the sun*
> *Whether near to me or far*
> *It's no matter darling where you are,*
> *I think of you night and day.*

Isabel didn't enjoy the piano but was very keen on painting and drawing, neither of which she was very talented at, but she became immensely knowledgeable and when she grew up had her own art gallery. We were taught all the traditional home pursuits: cooking, sewing and running a large house. Belvoir was an enterprise as formidable as a luxury hotel. We catered for quantities of people of all denominations. The store rooms adjacent to the kitchens were crammed with delicacies such as crystallised violets. The staff lived in cottages on the estate and had often worked for the family for their whole lives. Our childhood was an object lesson in how to run a household.

A young lady's education was not deemed to be complete without travelling to the Continent. My Mother arranged for Isabel and me to spend a few months in Paris. We stayed in the Hotel George V in luxury and walked to the Métro every day with our governess, Mademoiselle Monet, who was indomitable despite being only two thumbs high. We had always had French nursery maids at home but now were expected to speak French all the time, which meant there were quite a lot of sullen silences and secret whisperings. Tramping up and down the Champs-Elysées for hours, she walked us off our legs and I think we visited every museum in Paris, as well as the palaces at Saint-Germain and Malmaison.

Isabel used to complain but I loved our expeditions and especially remember going as far afield as Mont St Michel in Brittany, where we lunched in a restaurant at a table set with eight plates each for the eight different courses. Isabel, who loved food, could not get over it. It almost made up for her rebellion against Mademoiselle Monet's strictness. At a time when we were wildly curious about the physical side of love and wanting to read every novel we could lay our hands on, she banned *Wuthering Heights*, fearing that the unbridled passion of Heathcliff and Cathy might be infectious.

As a young girl my impression of Paris was of immense glamour. We had little awareness of the political trouble brewing in Europe: Mussolini in Italy, Hitler in Germany. After Paris I went on to Italy where I spent nine months at the Villa Malatesta, via Foscolo 56, Florence. Nowhere in the world did I walk as much as my finishing school in Florence, which was owned by Mrs Lestrange. Isabel was left at home as she was deemed still too young, but I travelled out on the train with my mother and father, even though I hadn't wanted to go to Italy and was terribly homesick and miserable at first. For me it was a huge change because I had never been to school of any kind, but always had private tuition. I felt shy and nervous, and a bit estranged from the other girls: I was aware they were much better educated than me. They were also physically stronger. I struggled with the steep walk from the Duomo up the hill along via Foscolo every day, giggling at the carabinieri. It made me aware that I didn't feel so at home with my own generation but gravitated to my elders, with whom I felt more comfortable.

Gradually the beauty around me began to infiltrate my soul and I realised I mustn't waste this wonderful opportunity. The fact that I had grown up surrounded by fine art and architecture meant I was able to appreciate it deeply. We had lectures every day and had to write endless essays – even the homework was a novelty for me. I was fascinated by the wonders of Florence and won a prize for an essay on the Ghiberti bronze doors of the Baptistery. We walked everywhere in twos in a crocodile formation until we were utterly exhausted. The carabinieri were astonished by these regimented young ladies. We had fun ragging them and spoiling their Mussolini pomp.

We studied the art and architecture further afield in San Gimignano, Siena and Rome, and saw the beautiful church with a tomb by Jacopo della Quercia in Lucca. We climbed the Leaning Tower in Pisa, all the while speaking Italian all day until 5pm – that was silence-making in itself. There were professors who visited from outside for dancing and I had a wonderful piano teacher called Signor Brugnoli, so for that period I learned a lot. At one stage I felt ill and Mrs Lestrange called in a doctor, a neat little short man with a beard, who proceeded to withdraw a lawn handkerchief from his breast pocket. Rather alarmingly he placed it against my bosom and listened to my heart. This was before the days of the stethoscope. Luckily I recovered quickly, no thanks to his ministrations.

At the same time there was a steady stream of people visiting from England, beseeched by my parents to drop in and see how I was doing. I felt rather shoved into meeting people like the art connoisseur Bernard Berenson, who lived at I Tatti, near Florence. He really put me through my paces and quizzed me about Renaissance art. Fortunately I managed to answer all his questions, upon which he announced he was writing to my parents to inform them I had acquitted myself satisfactorily. The food in Italy was delicious: we used to say it gave us 'l'acqualina in bocca' (literally mouthwatering). In the castle I was used to nursery food, bread and butter pudding and boiled potatoes. Now I discovered veal with garlic mushrooms, pasta with intensely flavourful sauces and an orange flavoured chestnut purée called Mont Blanc.

My father wrote to me from Belvoir on 2nd October 1933.

My darling,

I loved the arrival of your letter – but sorry to hear that have been having colds – but that is better than glandular fever – which is the filthiest disease I have come across – Poor little Johnnie – it is now three weeks and his temperature still goes up high – Anyhow yesterday we brought him up in an ambulance from that bloody place Westgate to Avenue Road and he was none the worse for the journey – he is now in your bedroom: and Mamma and I are so much happier now that he is in London near good doctors. I have very little news to give you except that I have been dashing between London and Westgate for the last two weeks – Can you picture me and Mamma squatting over our gas fire in the bedroom – having every ¾ of an hour to put 1/- in a slot to keep the gas going – and then going off to that filthy school to see poor Johnnie who has been frightfully ill – the night he had to have an operation on his throat to cut an abscess – but on the whole I think he is better – I have come down here today Friday to prepare a little shoot for Charles who comes down tomorrow with Mamma for his long leave.

Roger and Isabel here and both well.

I am longing for you to see the picture of Mamma hung up here – it is coming down here

*from Dame Laura's one day next week – and it
will then be varnished – the old Haddon frame
is ready for it – and it is to be hung for the time
being in the Ball Room – filling up the arch
behind the screen.*

*All my love to you my darling – I am so glad
you are hard at your piano and that you are
enjoying it – It will be lovely to get you to play to
me this Xmas.*

Goodbye old girl for the moment.

Papa

The painting by Dame Laura Knight which
Father mentions is a portrait of my mother which
he commissioned in the same style as the portrait of
Christina of Denmark, Duchess of Milan, by Hans
Holbein the Younger. My mother was wearing a long
slender sequinned dress with a huge snow-white
fox cape. Dame Laura came to stay at Haddon and
painted it in the Long Gallery where Dorothy Vernon
escaped. I imagine it must have been challenging
for her as we would all drop by and offer advice,
including my formidable grandmother Violet. The
portrait is now hanging in the picture gallery at
Belvoir. Laura had done marvellous drawings of
Diaghilev's Ballet Russes and had befriended many
of the dancers, including Pavlova, Karsavina and
Massine. Later she worked backstage with the Royal

Shakespeare Company at Stratford. She was the first female artist to become a full member of the Royal Academy and to become a Dame. We became close friends and I have kept the charming letters – littered with impulsive drawings – which she sent me from 16 Langford Place in St John's Wood. One dated 28th April 1953 exhorted me to go to the Royal Academy to see 'I believe some of my best work'.

Mrs Keppel, the mistress of King Edward VII, had retired to a cottage at the bottom of the garden of Berenson's Villa, I Tatti. She wrote to my father saying: 'I have Sidney Herbert staying with me and he would be a marvellous match for Ursula. I have written to the school to invite her over for lunch or dinner but they won't allow it without a letter of authorisation from you'. She knew my parents wanted me to marry someone from my world. Sadly the letter didn't come in time as I only stayed for two terms and rather regret that now. On the way home to England I was put in the charge of the guard and travelled alone, which made me feel very grown up. Later in London I did meet Sidney Herbert, who became the 16th Earl of Pembroke, but there was no spark there. He was always interested in art and when he inherited Wilton House, wrote a scholarly catalogue of the paintings in his collection.

Chapter Three
Coming Out

In 1934 when I turned seventeen a ball was given at Belvoir for me and my sister. Our coming out dresses were from Worth in Paris. We were dressed as twins in white tulle layered dresses with tiny short sleeves and wide green silk sashes, and shod in white satin shoes. We felt disappointed because we thought they didn't look very grown up – which we felt we were now – but we didn't have any choice in the matter. We forgot our disappointment with the thrill of the ball where we stood at the top of the stairs and greeted our guests, easily over two hundred people. All the local families and friends thronged the castle. We had many, many boyfriends and danced to the band until all hours. Despite our feeling of being terribly grown up and sophisticated, neither Isabel nor I at the age of seventeen had any idea where babies came from. I was still the same girl with hairy legs whom my ruthless younger brothers Johnny and Roger would chase around the room shouting: 'Shaving brush, old girl!'

Father gave me a heart-shaped brooch he had designed himself – a huge pale aquamarine with a garter ribbon and my name written in diamonds. I really minded when it was stolen in a big raid on Carrington's, the family jewellers in London, where we would just push our jewels over the counter the morning after we had worn them. I do think the only way to keep your jewellery safe is to have an Edwardian chest with secret drawers. I like to wear a few pieces of jewellery with sentimental value but otherwise too much is not advisable and should be saved for grand occasions.

Suddenly I was launched on the world and expected to be a young lady with great social graces, and dressed immaculately in the most beautiful clothes. Society in those days set a standard of elegance and intellectual ability which was daunting to a young girl who had spent most of her life at home and had never seen anyone much other than her cousins. Everyone seemed to have a political arrogance not seen today, frightening for a naive young lady. Men started to appear in my world. My first kiss was from one of father's friends in my beautiful bedroom at Belvoir. He was much older than me, so it came as a total surprise when he embraced me. He clutched me gently against his cheek, holding my chin and putting his tongue in my mouth. He must have had a shock and realised just how young and inexperienced I was because I jumped. He made three enchanting remarks and left in a hurry. I was seventeen and he was fifty. I was in a state of bewilderment. On reflection I decided I must be something exceptional with excessive appeal to the opposite sex. I had the pick of the most fascinating young men in England, but I looked upon them as boys like my brothers at Eton. In fact I was besotted not with my contemporaries but with older men, and from that moment on nothing was to be the same again.

One of the most fantastically beautiful houses in the vicinity was Belton, a 17th century masterpiece with all its original furniture, tapestries and magnificent silver, only ten miles away from Belvoir, four miles outside Grantham. Here they entertained in a grand way. The owner was Lord Brownlow (Perry), a friend of father's who was in the Prince of Wales' set. Perry was the one who took the Duke of Windsor to France after the scandal of the abdication. He was married to a Kinloch from Scotland who was very pretty but not the sort to settle in the country. He lived at Belton on his own. (His son eventually gave Belton to the National Trust and went off to live in Paris).

He hosted the most risqué dinner parties which were not the sort of thing a child like myself should have been allowed to go to, just having been launched on the world. With my chaperones got rid of I was free and had no grown-up to answer to. I was asked to spend the weekend at this dream house and fate took its toll. I was the only young person there with luxurious wine and food in a dining room of great beauty festooned with orchids in silver dishes, a level of grandeur I had rarely seen. Outside the house was an orangery, stables and a courtyard with long avenues stretching across the deer park. The custom was that the ladies left the gentlemen to their port and garrulous conversation.

Perry introduced me to the biggest roué in the world, Lord Wimborne, who used to take me out. He was great company, highly intelligent with a ripping sense of humour. Perry used to come back now and again to Belton and all his friends would appear from their clubs in London, all the old blades. The girls would flock to their parties and I was no exception.

When I came out there was a sudden burst of freedom which was exhilarating, after being heavily chaperoned for years. I felt as free as a bird and could go out anywhere and stay with whomever I wanted. Isabel didn't come out until the following year as she was younger. She ran off with Loel Guinness, the heir to the banking branch of the brewery dynasty, an

MP who was previously married with a young son. Loel had divorced his first wife, Joan Yarde-Buller, sensationally naming Prince Aly Khan, son and heir of the Aga Khan, as co-respondent and gaining custody of their sons. There were headlines in the papers: LOEL GUINNESS WEDS LADY ISABEL MANNERS; Daughter of Duke and Duchess of Rutland Becomes Bride of British MP. November 1936.

My father and mother were absolutely dumbfounded, but she was longing to get away from home and that kind of life. She didn't know what love was, and she was even younger than me. They went on the longest honeymoon that has ever been, so long that it wasn't insured by Lloyd's. They sailed for over four months on their yacht, Atlantis, to Palm Beach and New York. So I went alone to all the huge parties and had five years of growing up in the most enjoyable way. I truly regret my sister never had that experience.

When the Prince of Wales abdicated, my father refused to have him in the house. Even though he had hunted with us many times at Belvoir he was shocked at the betrayal of the country, as my father and mother were great friends of his brother Bertie and his young wife Elizabeth. After the war I did meet Mrs Simpson in the South of France. A great friend of mine, Arthur Forbes, who later became

Lord Granard, was invited to dinner with the Duke and Duchess of Windsor and asked me along. It was the grandest thing you could imagine. The house had marble steps down to the front door and on every second step stood a coloured footman in royal livery. They were part of her retinue which she had brought back from the Bahamas where the Duke had been Governor. We sat down twenty-four people for dinner. Mrs Simpson was sitting next to an eminent member of the French government and I was one seat away. She spoke perfect French and was very witty: I hadn't realised how bright she was. After dinner we were whisked off to the casino in Cannes and I ended up sitting next to the Duke. He was wearing a Scottish kilt and when he produced a fabulous gold cigarette case it had a tinder with matching tartan. We chatted about hunting in Leicestershire and all the while she glared at us. He was very nice, not particularly amusing and completely controlled by her. She suddenly interjected: 'You had better have your special whisky now,' and produced a hunting flask in the middle of the casino.

Chapter Four
Maid of Honour

The months leading up to the coronation of George VI on 12th May 1937 were the pinnacle of excitement. I can remember every detail as if it was yesterday. The decorations in London were extraordinary. Bond Street was lit up with hundreds of vertical banners with gold crowns at the top – simple but magical. Selfridge's had all the flags flying and 'God Save the King' above the doors at the main entrance. At Piccadilly Circus there were dozens of red poles festooned with banners showing the royal crest and 'G and E' for George and Elizabeth, and gold crowns on the top. In Regent Street the red poles had panels with pictures of angels, topped off with red and white circular strips like barber's poles, and more gold crowns on the top. Whitehall, Kensington Palace and Westminster Abbey were all lit up at night.

All my family were involved in the coronation. My father carried the orb in the procession into the Abbey. My mother, as Duchess of Rutland, was a canopy-bearer to the Queen, along with three other duchesses, Buccleuch, Roxburghe and Norfolk. There is a beautiful portrait of my mother by Drion wearing her Hartnell gown. I have the matching one of my father in my flat. My brother Charles was Page of Honour to the Duke of Gloucester and my younger brother was Page of Honour to Lord Ancaster, the Lord Great Chamberlain. The boys wore breeches and jackets in bright colours. And I, wearing a fitted, white satin, puffed sleeved Norman Hartnell gown, with motif of corn embroidered in paillettes all the down the front, was a Maid of Honour to the Queen. There were six of us chosen and we were dressed identically. We had matching tiaras and wore only light powder and lipstick which we applied ourselves.

I felt so honoured and happy to be with friends: my first cousin Lady Elizabeth Paget, Marjorie Anglesey's daughter; Peggy, the Duke of Portland's granddaughter, and Lady Elizabeth Percy. Elizabeth was the daughter of the Duchess of Northumberland, who acted as Mistress of Robes to the Queen. The Duchess was very tall and regal, and looked very much the part, nearly six feet high. She accompanied the Queen at every stage of the proceedings. Princess Marina of Kent, Princess Alexandra's mother, looked especially beautiful. The colours and the music of the coronation in Westminster and the screaming crowds were overwhelming. Despite the very complicated logistics there wasn't a hitch and it went like clockwork.

The rehearsal was fascinating. When we had to go to the altar the space was very restricted and I was right behind one of the bishops. We were told very precisely what to do but Queen Elizabeth didn't even listen. She just did what she thought was the best and nobody dared to say anything. What was exciting was the crowds and the unbelievable noise. They were waiting all day, and the roar when the gold carriage passed by was deafening. Thousands of people crammed the streets and perched in the trees, dressed up to the nines. I suppose after the ghastly time of the Great War, the Depression and the Abdication, this was the release of folly; music and wonder prevailed. The whole of London was en fête and wherever you went you saw people drinking, singing, eating in the streets.

The Maids of Honour varied in height. My cousin Lady Elizabeth Paget was very tall and I was one of the shortest, which is why I was in the front. It was such excitement being on the balcony of Buckingham Palace, carrying the Queen's huge, ermine-trimmed velvet train, which weighed such a lot she couldn't dress without our help or the whole equipage being taken off. We didn't have loops to hold the train; rather there were openings in the seam, into which you had to slide your hand. We were terrified of dropping it and, because of nerves, became rather giggly. As the train was attached to the Queen we had to follow her round in the Palace. When finally we emerged onto the balcony I was standing next to the Queen, the King's mother, Queen Mary, and behind the young Princesses Elizabeth and Margaret. Three generations of Queens all together. At the end of that magical day we were sent home from Buckingham Palace in a taxi, overwhelmed by what we had been through.

A certain Mr Laurence McKinney from Albany, New York wrote to *The Knickerbocker Press* on Tuesday 25th May 1937:

Ballade of Inquiry
In many of the pictures of the coronation there is shown back of the royal party a statuesque brunette with a widow's peak. Who is she? London papers please copy.

Glittering pictures from over the sea
Giving the scenes of yesterweek,
Pictures of pomp and panoply
Show of the century, vast, unique,
Here is royalty, cheek to cheek

With pompous peers of the highest rating,
But who is that Girl with the Widow's Peak?

Who is that beautiful Lady in Waiting?
Rumbling from early history
Trumpeters tootle and coaches creak,
Bishops perform with solemnity
(Though Princess may yawn and Princess may tweak)
Cheers for his Majesty, mild and meek!
Cheers for his consort, dominating!
But who is that Girl with the Widow's Peak?

Who is that beautiful Lady in Waiting?
Pageants are duller for you and me
Frankly we find them a little bleak,
Movies have featured them, endlessly,
And Hollywood heroes are nice and sleek,
Cinema ladies are always chic –
That is a fact that there's no debating –
But who is that Girl with the Widow's Peak?

Who is that beautiful Lady in Waiting?
News photographers, prithee speak,
Quiet these hearts that are palpitating.
Say, who is that Girl with the Widow's Peak?
Who is that beautiful Lady in Waiting?

It was a story that ran for several days until the Editor eventually replied:

Personal Note, Addressed solely to Mr McKinney

Dear Mr McKinney

We gathered that you desired us to set some discreet inquiries afoot as to the identity of the girl with the widow's peak in question. Accordingly, we have done so, and are pleased to report that we are sending herewith the information which we believe you were seeking.

We regret that there has been some slight delay in obtaining the information, owing to the unusual nature of the inquiry. The matter was referred promptly to our Pictures of Pomp and Panoply Department, and after investigation by them was routed through the Pompous Peers Department, thence to the Palpitating Hearts Editor. The latter acted immediately, putting the question directly up to our Associated Press Photos man at New York. The cable to London crackled, or whatever cables do.

Attached herewith is the wire which we have just received from our man.

Managing Editor Knickerbocker Press Albany NY – GIRL IN CORONATION PIX IS LADY URSULA MANNERS. SORRY DELAY

IN IDENTIFYING. AP PHOTOS.
We trust the above is satisfactory and we are
happy to have been of service to you.
Yours very truly
Jo Leonard.

After the coronation I was recognised everywhere and had a sort of awakening. I was suddenly popular, and this produced a lot of jealousy amongst my peers. All the time I was nearly unconscious with fear and nerves, trying not to appear too grand. I may have seemed austere, but it was only because I was terrified. If you are spoiled to that degree from birth you are doomed, but it was just the way it was. The famous Duchess who built Belvoir Castle nearly bankrupted the place and my father was stretched to the limit. The estate and money went to the eldest boy, girls never had any money. I had no money of my own and was brought up to be subservient to the male species. I realised from birth that I was expected to marry a duke in due course. I felt I should have been a boy, and that's why father took me everywhere, as though I was going to inherit. I was his eldest child and shared his interests, working with him in the restoration of Haddon.

After the coronation I accompanied my Mother and Aunt Diana Cooper and Duff, her husband, and Winston Churchill and his wife on the first visit to

Paris of the new King and Queen on 19th July 1938. They went at the invitation of the French government and the Président de la République, Monsieur Lebrun. My father couldn't come for some reason and I was so lucky to be included. When the train arrived at Bois de Boulogne station we disembarked into a remarkable pavilion which had been especially constructed for the visit. The Champs-Elysées was solid with humanity. There were thousands of people screaming: 'Why don't we have a Queen?' There were tapestries hanging in the streets and flowers and feathers everywhere. The French laid on the most lavish entertainment. I suppose they wanted to prove they had tanks and so we went to a military parade. When the tanks appeared they had flags of all the suits in sets of cards. Churchill was so excited we had to hold on to him by his coat tails.

There was a State Visit to the Opera and I will always remember the Queen standing on the steps of the Opera while a cortège of hundreds of soldiers in a guard riding beautiful Arab horses galloped flat out towards us and then suddenly stopped dead still. The main horse was wearing a ram's head in gold as a mascot. It was the most sensational and terrifying thing I had ever seen. Winston kept saying: 'Where's the cygnet?' and my mother would say, 'Don't worry'. That was his nickname for me as I was the youngest in the party.

The most lavish event was our visit to Versailles. Firstly we saw an al fresco ballet in the glorious setting of the gardens, featuring the future Hollywood star Zizi Jeanmaire and choreographed by her husband Roland Petit. We were then escorted into the Galérie des Glaces for lunch. There were dozens of footmen, one standing behind each seat, wearing 18th century uniforms. At the end of the table I sat next to a very old man, Monsieur Flandins, who was an expert in antiquities. He gave everyone a medal to commemorate the occasion – gold for Their Majesties and bronze for the rest of us. He didn't like the British and made that quite clear, so I just sat in silence admiring my medal, swallowing the food and staring at the wonder of it all. I had learned enough French to understand nearly everything although I couldn't speak much. In my school-days I thought I could get by and now realise I should have worked harder at French and Italian. Nobody regrets it more.

London returned the hospitality to Président Lebrun and his wife when they came to London in March 1939. On 22nd March they attended a Gala performance of Sleeping Beauty starring a young Margot Fonteyn at the Royal Opera House in Covent Garden. We were all seated in the Dress Circle, the façade of which had been designed by Rex Whistler. Rex wrote to me on 27th January 1937.

20 Fitzer's Street W1
Thursday night

My beautiful Ursie,

Will you go to a movie with me on Thursday evening and have some supper? As I implored you to do on the telephone last week and you practically said you would? I wouldn't make you go in my 'open sports' (unless it's a blazing hot night, thick with stars and moths and moonlight).

If you can't go to the movie on Thursday then I order you, at the very least, to come and have a fireside tea with me in my studio – where, incidentally, you haven't been since you were a tiny child of about twelve, have you?

I will regale you with soft ravishing music from my lovely (human) skin coloured American gramophone (and guaranteed no record later than 1935).

Alas I can't come to Belvoir for next weekend. I'm so terribly busy that it simply is not possible for me to take the time off then. I've already begun the vast Plas.N. work in my new studio! at Lambeth: will you come one day and look it over after lunch?

Longing to see you (and counting upon seeing you, what's more).

64

I wish I could come to Belvoir, it was so sweet
of you to ask me.
Love from Rex.

In November 2012 I went to an exhibition called The Unseen Rex Whistler in the famous Yellow Room at Colefax & Fowler at 39 Brook Street, Mayfair. It was held to launch a new biography of Rex *In Search of Rex Whistler* by Hugh and Mirabel Cecil, published by Frances Lincoln. It was a joy to see his wonderful portrait of my cousin Caroline Anglesey as well as eight previously unseen murals he painted at 19 Hill Street, Mayfair for Mrs Euan Wallace, daughter of Sir Edwin Lutyens. In his tragically short life he truly paved the way for the Neo-Romanticists.

Back in London there were several older men in my life. After having been heavily chaperoned until 1934, I did not know how to cope with so many people running after me. The change was so sudden. I had been so sheltered previously. In those five years before the war you could choose between four great balls every night, rivalling each other in luxury and grandeur. The waltz was my favourite dance. I had been presented at Court in 1936 to Queen Mary and King George V, wearing white and with feathers in my hair. I learned the drill – how to curtsey and walk backwards – from Mrs Vacani, who taught everyone. There was a Court Ball every summer to which one was bidden. London tingled. There was little general premonition of the tragedies and disasters that were soon to unfold.

There were wonderful weekend parties organised for the young people at country houses like Cliveden. Lady Astor kept open house for the young and Bill Astor was a great friend of mine. My brothers were at Eton and she used to entertain nearly the whole school there as it was so close. For Ascot Racing and the Derby people dressed up to the nines but it was so snobby then that only selected people were allowed into the Royal Enclosure.

I loved being invited by my aunt Lady Diana Cooper. She entertained with great flair the most famous people from all over the world and you were honoured to be asked. She was my father's younger sister and was famed for her beauty. She appeared in all the magazines in the latest fashions, which she adored. As an actress she had starred in Max Reinhart's *The Miracle*. She was very nice to me but used to tick me off because I didn't really care about the way I looked. She would say: 'Darling, it's all very well being a wild child in the garden and playing at Mrs Mop, but it's very selfish because other people have to look at you'. She was immensely encouraging and flattering if you did something well or your house was beautiful. She tried to give me tips about being a good hostess: 'Darling, you must always have a round table because then those who want to talk can, while the quiet ones can listen'.

Her husband, Duff Cooper, who was to be created Viscount Norwich in 1952, was a prominent British Conservative party politician and diplomat. His friendship at Eton with John Manners won him entry into a fashionable circle of young aristocrats and intellectuals known as the Coterie with Raymond Asquith, which was where he met and fell in love with Diana. He served with distinction in the Grenadier Guards and became an MP. He was elevated to the Cabinet as War Secretary in 1935 and promoted to First Lord of the Admiralty in 1937. He was the most public critic of Chamberlain's policy of appeasement and famously resigned the day after the 1938 Munich Agreement was made with Hitler.

He was a prolific author and wrote a marvellous book on Talleyrand. To me he seemed rather spoiled and certainly didn't suffer fools gladly. He would rush off and play bridge after dinner if the conversation was less than brilliant. If a woman was beautiful he could be fascinating, but if she was rather plain he would just sit like a lump.

For a weekend with Lord Dudley at Himley Hall in Staffordshire, his exquisite 18th and early 19th century house, I was driven in the family car with the chauffeur and a lady's maid, who was usually French or Italian to improve my language skills. For just one weekend a whole trunkful of glamorous clothes would be packed, along with some of the pretty ornaments and pictures from home to decorate my bedroom. What was charming was that younger and older people all mingled. We would be welcomed into the sympathetic library, a room both formal and cosy. After unpacking and a big lunch we would swim in the pool inside the house, play golf or tennis or just lie in the sun. Some played bridge in a very high fashioned way but I was never good enough to compete. I was quite content playing billiard fives and having fun on the tennis court. It didn't seem to matter that I was quite hopeless. Our host Eric Dudley was a famous businessman and a Director of the Railways.

Every night we wore long gowns with abundant jewellery for dinner and the gentlemen were in white tie. Everybody went to church on Sunday mornings, including the servants who would come straight from the kitchen, still wearing their aprons. After lunch we would all walk in the gardens, which were spectacular. The entire display you would see now in a London florist shop would have been the arrangement at the bottom of the stairs.

We had wonderful times too at Chatsworth which was just 'over the garden wall' from Haddon, and fantastic parties in Scotland at Drumlanrig Castle with the Buccleuchs, with the Colquhouns at Hyndford, North Berwick, and with Tennant relations at Ross-Dhu, which is now a famous golf links. Nearly all the families had eldest sons who were my age, which was fun. Of course we also had our family obligations and I had to play my part at home, opening bazaars and helping with the Girl Guides.

The Duchess of Alba, Cayetana Fitz-James Stuart y Silva, invited me to Seville in October 1947 for her wedding. I was very excited to go to Spain and travelled with a Spanish girlfriend, the Marchese de Naros. The wedding took place in Seville Cathedral and you cannot imagine a more glorious sight than all the guests wearing fantastic designs by Balenciaga and glittering with jewels. I wore a black lace dress with red bows which I had made myself, inspired by the paintings of Goya, and a beautiful mantilla. The whole of Seville was alight. The noise was such as though castanets were being played by every child in Spain.

When we walked back through the crowds to the Palacio de las Dueñas, the Seville palace of the Alba family, for the reception I was cheered more than the Duchess, which was a little embarrassing. That was her first wedding. At the age of eighty-five she has just got married for the third time, contrary to the wishes of her six children, to Alfonso Diez, aged a mere sixty.

I used to have clothes made up by a dressmaker and sometimes Hartnell would let me have a dress for the night as I was his model's size six. For special events Mother would take me to Worth, who made the most exquisite dresses. We used to go to the hairdresser next door called Antoine. Worth made me a gold sequinned dress which I wore when I went with my father to a fashionable dinner given by Lady Cunard in her house in Piccadilly. The dress was so sophisticated and more suited to a married woman than a young girl, but I loved it. Emerald was very wicked and used to pick on people. Everyone was talking about Rhodesia and she interrupted and said: 'Even the latest will know all about Cecil Rhodes', and of course I was woefully ignorant. My father laughed and so did I. Then the war came like a knife going into a piece of butter and changed society completely.

Chapter Five
We will never lunch at this table again

In 1939 we were all sitting having lunch in the Banqueting Hall at Haddon Hall when Father said: 'I want everyone to listen. We will never lunch at this table again. War has been declared'. It was a terrible shock to us all and we sat in absolute silence. Many people at the table had been in the First World War, as had my father and mother, so altogether we were very grim. My mother had lost her favourite brother in the First World War and had three sons who would be eligible to fight. One eventually joined the SAS and could hardly come in the front door, so accustomed was he to coming in the window.

My father immediately left Haddon and went to Belvoir and managed to communicate with all the right people in government. He arranged to lend Belvoir and Haddon as a repository during the duration of the war for all the important historic national documents from the Public Record office. In a few weeks time masses of trucks turned up with, it seemed, half the British Museum and national libraries packed in huge crates, accompanied by curators. I believe the Doomsday Book was among these valuable works. Everything had to be stored so carefully and at the right temperature and it was all perfectly looked after. All the experts running these departments for the government were housed in the castle or nearby and took over the maintenance of the castle. My father was appointed a Curator of the Public Record Office, as the official guardian of these national treasures. My father showed great foresight because it was a way of looking after the place, as the government had to ensure there were no leaks or damp, and everything was kept immaculately clean. He did not want the castle turned into a hospital, barracks or a school, which would have knocked it about too much.

As the bombs started to fall on London my father died of septicaemia on 22nd April 1940. He was only fifty-three and his death was traumatic for me as I absolutely worshipped him. When I was a child he would come and sit by my side when I was sick, like a lover. I think that is why I always liked older men. His doctor, Lord Dawson of Penn, was also the King's doctor, and when Father was lying on his death bed this wretched doctor came, and called me to say: 'You had better come and see your dead father'. I nearly passed out with shock. My father used to go to all these extraordinary places in Egypt and was always picking up bugs. He used to inject himself with antibodies but never seemed ill to me. He had just finished restoring Haddon, which had been an enormously pleasurable task for him, and I could not believe he was gone.

I feel I must break my narrative here by writing a little more about my wonderful father. Looking back over my life, he was also mother, lover, friend, everything you could imagine, and when he died at just over the age of fifty it really was the end of it all for me for quite a while. From my early childhood he used to come and talk to me every evening in bed. For most children their mother would read to them at bedtime, but for me it was the opposite. If I was ill he would bring me up a jug of champagne and say: 'Cheer up, you will be all right in the morning'.

He used to expect one to be always very, very clean and immaculately dressed, especially in the drawing room part of the house. He taught all of us to respect fine furniture, and never to put a wet glass on a lovely mahogany top. He encouraged me to observe everything in the outside world of politics and in the interior world of the Castle. In those days a duke was like a king in his territory, which was vast and self-supporting. I suppose he treated me as though I was a son and was going to inherit, or maybe he loved me because I was pretty, cosy and dreamy – quite the opposite of my more vivacious and acerbic sister. I used to follow him round like a puppy, content to be in his shadow and give him a helping hand whenever I could, whereas Isabel and Charles were more of a liability and were often up to something very naughty.

There was never a dull moment with my father. He was extremely modern while steeped in tradition and maintaining some of the old fashioned ways. As I grew up he initiated me slowly into driving a car, despite some hairy moments while I was learning. When I turned seventeen he took me to Drummond's Bank in Charing Cross to open my first bank account. I was very impressed that Father was dressed in a frock coat with a gardenia in his buttonhole. It turned out that was his natural clothing for his business life in London. I was delighted that the bank manager bowed deeply to me and then ushered us into his private office. I still bank there today.

Father was always in and out of the Ritz. He was also a member of the Bath Club at 34 Dover Street, where I learned to swim. This involved a rather intimidating procedure of getting into the shallow end and then waiting for an old lady to throw out a bamboo pole which you had to try and swim to reach. I did eventually receive a hard won medal.

The Castle was always full of very amusing people, mostly from the political world, whom Mother enjoyed entertaining. Father joined in and was an admirable host, but his great passion was for his own private pursuits. His collections of antique tiles and rare birds' eggs were unique. In an extraordinary way he was fascinated by the archaeological discoveries at Pompeii and Herculaneum. He and my mother went with Carter and Carnavon to the opening of the Tutankhamun Exhibition. He dug up the early monastery at Croston on the Belvoir Estate and discovered how it all functioned in the very earliest days. He found one particular sarcophagus with a full length figure of Lord Roos, engraved in stone with lead eyes which enabled historians to date it. This caused an absolute furore.

My father used to design jewellery and made some lovely pieces. On my seventeenth birthday, when I came out, he gave me a brooch with a mammoth jewel, the palest of aquamarines set in a deep cut setting surrounded by garter blue enamel crossed at the bottom, with my name in diamonds written in tiny letters. He was such a clever designer and I would have loved to have kept his drawings, but after the war Carrington's, the jewellers in Regent Street, was taken over by another firm and everything was lost.

He wrote me little notes almost daily, and introduced a telephone to great excitement. If a call came in, the porter would ask a footman to rush around and find the right person with a message to come to the phone. The porter's lodge was the centre of operations, like a concierge's desk in an hotel. My father introduced me to how to look at paintings, as he had been taught by my grandmother, who was a famous sculptor. He enjoyed the company of his few men friends, who shared his love of fishing and shooting, and the resident vicar, the Reverend Mr Knox, who took services in the chapel every Sunday. The Vicar had a grace-and-favour house in Knipton, a village on the estate. He shot and fished and tried to make the boys good and true, know the Lord's Prayer and Catechism, and became a great personal friend in whom they could confide.

He was a very warm, charming and heavenly father. I loved him and so did most of the people on the estate who had been there all their lives. He was very conscious of elegance – it didn't matter what people wore during the day but men were expected to wear white tie in the evening. If my boyfriends came to stay and didn't have one, they would hurry to the footman to borrow one. After dinner when the ladies went out and the gentlemen stayed at the table to drink port he was in his element. He was particularly fond of his brother-in-law, Duff Cooper, and was a whiz at high stakes poker.

Although he would often go to stay in Taunton with a friend nothing really counted in the same way as his work. Nothing interrupted his breakfast and his work. I don't think he told anybody for years how he was suffering. When he died I found quite a few hypodermic syringes which I believe he used for pain relief. In those days you always had a tame doctor who would do what you wanted, as well as what was good for you. He disliked hunting; he liked the dogs but couldn't bear the horses. And he thought the people who hunted at Melton were immoral and sinister, a drunken and vulgar crowd who surrounded the Prince of Wales. He never wanted Isabel and me to hang out with that crowd, but sometimes we used to escape and go to parties, putting bolsters in our bed to conceal our absence.

There were lovely kennels in the immediate vicinity of the castle which he used to keep in a very model, up-to-date way. Although we had stables, he would refer our guests to the Peacock Pub to stable their horses, which is now the Dower House. Our uncle Edward Tennant, my mother's brother, always stayed there because he liked hunting. He was famous as the fellow who flew over Baghdad in the First World War and wrote a book called *Above the Clouds of Baghdad: Being the Records of an Air*

Commander (1920). He survived the war, while her younger brother, Mark, whom she adored, was killed.

When I look back, I think Father died at the right time. He would have been utterly miserable in the modern world. He was used to his footmen dressed in livery, and the entire gardens, dairy, kitchen and upholstery shops, the stables tack-room filled with silver mounted livery, all at full throttle in the castle, and run like a cross between a luxury hotel, a museum and a theatre. He had all his rituals, such as the little walk down from the chapel to the dairy on Sunday mornings to test the cheeses.

On his death, Mother was struck with horror at getting to grips with the administration and financial work he had always looked after. His secretary, Mr Alders, had joined up and become Montgomery's secretary and never returned to Belvoir. In a turmoil of grief we moved from the castle to what was the Peacock Hotel at the bottom of the hill. It was a small pub and hotel with a stable yard which was popular for hunting weekends. We made it into a lovely family home which we called The Lodge and lived there for the duration. It had many bedrooms, a dear dining room and a drawing room which opened onto a pretty garden which Mother created. At the back was a yard with a lot of horse boxes for people who came for the hunt. It certainly made a warm welcome for the boys who came home from the war. Suddenly the soldiers would arrive and it would become a centre of drunken fun and folly.

Mother's old Scottish cook performed daily miracles of conjuring up meals for many people out of the least possible food. Sad to say, the dairy and kitchen garden were left to the care of one old man and gradually deteriorated. Most hunting ceased in the war, except for Lord Knaresborough, because there were no whippers-in and the dogs run away. The Belvoir hounds were kept in the kennels and we kept some countryside skills going. However, sometimes the hounds were lost because nobody could keep up with them after the fox as there were few followers. If you were lucky enough to have a horse you had the best hunting in the world because you could just go flat out.

The gardener's wife, Mrs Stubley, helped teach us to look after the fifteen bee hives which we moved from the castle gardens. This was a huge effort when the racks were full of honey, but it meant we were lucky enough to have a source of sugar all through the war. I became fascinated by the bees and the famous book, *Life of the Bee*, by Maeterlinck. After the war I saw an advertisement in a specialist bee magazine for a queen bee from Italy. Italian bees were reputed to be more docile than the little British black bees. Her Majesty duly arrived through the post in a perforated matchbox, none the worse for her travels.

After Father's death, Mother was distraught and had to face a new life alone, while all the time desperately worried about my three brothers who were at the Front. Fortunately they did return safely. My eldest brother Charles had been shot in the foot but survived and recuperated at home with her.

All the girls I knew joined up to help the war effort and I became a VAD. The Voluntary Aid Detachment had been set up by the Red Cross in 1909 and had provided nursing assistance during the First World War. I went to stay in Mother's house in Audley Square, proudly wearing my white uniform with a red cross on the front. My first posting was to the Ashton Hotel in Paddington where we cleaned railway carriages until we dropped. We were told the authorities were thinking of evacuating all of London. I was then sent to nurse at St George's Hospital at Hyde Park Corner, which is now the Lanesborough Hotel. The operating theatre was on the roof, which was clearly not convenient in wartime, so everything had to be restructured. I had to give atropine injections before an operation, having had barely any training. Our saving grace was that we were so busy and exhausted we didn't have time to be frightened. The flat white shoes we wore were good for running, and although we were supposed never to run in the hospital unless there was a haemorrhage, we seemed to be constantly in a rush.

After I finished nursing one night I came home paralytically tired and ready to collapse into bed. Our Spanish maid said she was going to sleep in the shelter in Hyde Park and I should come with her, or at least sleep in the basement where she had made up a bed for me. Every day I would say 'Not on your nelly'. I couldn't bear it as I was so exhausted and just flopped into my own bed. During the night the bombing was heavy and a huge blast came and took out the whole basement of the house. My room was above the front door and I was totally alone in the house. I hadn't heard a thing and the first thing I saw was a man's face right up close to mine. I couldn't believe it until he said: 'Don't scream, don't panic, don't get a dressing gown, just stealthily get out of bed and follow me without saying a word'. He was a policeman. So we crept out of this rather beautiful, very tall house, down the stone stairs, me shivering in my nightgown. We were lucky to get out before anything more collapsed and if I had been asleep in the basement I would certainly not have survived. He took me to the foyer of the Dorchester Hotel, which was reputed to be safe because it was made of steel and concrete. There were hundreds of people there in the strangest assortment of night and day clothes, carrying Pekineses, jewellery boxes and forlorn odd possessions. I knew that my Uncle Duff Cooper and Aunt Diana lived at the hotel and went down to the basement, where the guests were moved during raids, to try and find them. There were lots of families in the basement and I saw a screen in a corner with Cooper written in large letters, but didn't dare to wake them. I just sat in the foyer until daybreak in a state of shock.

Diana and Duff also lived during the war at my grandmother's little Sussex farmhouse at Aldwick, right on the edge of the English Channel near Bognor. The great thing before the war if one was ill had been to have sea air and Bognor was always full of amusing people at the weekend. The King and Queen went down there when he was ill and stayed in a big hotel. We were asked to play on the beach with the Princesses Elizabeth and Margaret. I found it very amusing watching the nannies dressed in stiff navy blue serge from head to foot paddling in the sea, still wearing their hats. When later on Lady Diana lived in the Aldwick farmhouse, there was just the old butler and one cow, but somehow they managed to produce delicious cheeses. She could improvise wonderful outfits and when she came to Belvoir at Christmas would arrive with dresses made from paper for us to act in charades every evening.

Duff and Diana's son, my cousin, John Julius Cooper, who was to succeed his father as 2nd Viscount Norwich in 1954, published in 2013 some of the letters his mother had written to him as a boy during the war. On 17th August 1940, when he was 10, she wrote 'Papa [his father, Duff Cooper] broadcast this evening. I couldn't hear it because I had a dinner party downstairs here [the Dorchester Hotel], thirty-two-strong, for overseas officers. I took my little receiving set to hold to my ear, but Ursula put it out of action by dropping it within five seconds of my asking her to hold it'.

On 11th September Diana 1940 wrote, 'Ursula came panting in early in the morning, pea-green in the face and utterly whacked, but grinning and cheerful. She is a nurse in Battersea Hospital and has had a gruelling time. She had not been to bed for three nights and the bombs had been clustering round them in their efforts to hit the power station. Last night a delayed action bomb fell beside them so all the patients had to be evacuated to another hospital, and once done she had twenty-four hours to rest. She's a fine good girl.' Then, four days later we read, 'Ursula rushed in to say her Battersea Hospital had folded up on her – too many bombs and delayed bombs strewn all around, so the patients were evacuated for good. She's going straight into St. George's tomorrow.'

After my narrow escape in the blitz with Duff and Diana at the Dorchester, I rang my mother and said I'd better collect all the family valuables I could from banks and jewellery shops. My Mother had really no idea of what was happening in the capital and said: 'Don't be silly, London is the safest place to be!' It was typical of the lack of communication there was in England at that time. I was desperate to get home and Lord Beaverbrook, whom I knew well, helped arrange some transport. I headed off to Carrington's in Regent Street to see my lovely old Mr Hughes, who looked after our family jewels, to rescue things and take them back to Belvoir. When I arrived home with the family tiara on my knee my Mother was surprised.

By the time the bombs started to fall in earnest the last thing the London doctors wanted was a bunch of giggly girls, who knew not much more than how to put on a bandage and stroke a fevered brow. They needed trained professional nurses so decided to ship the VADs off to country hospitals. I was determined not to and decided to go home and give up nursing. My mother was head of the British Red Cross for the county and I wanted to do something that mattered. I called on my friend old Perry Brownlow, who had been Mayor of Grantham. Perry introduced me to the Managing Director of the munitions factory BMARC, British Manufacture and Research Company. Mr Denis Kendall, who later became MP for Grantham, looked me up and down dubiously and finally said: 'I will find a job for you'. I became very friendly with Mr Kendall and sometimes would go to Blackpool with him to see his mother. She was an original and used to run peas off a knife into her mouth, which I had never seen. He was protective of me as I was still a child, but he had thrown me into this very responsible job.

The factory was on a sixty-acre site on Springfield Road in Grantham and made bullets for Oerlikon guns. There were 7,800 employees. The moment France fell this little subsidiary was in incredible demand because it made the bullets and shells. They had the same velocity as a machine gun but with an explosive tip, whereas the ordinary munitions didn't penetrate German armour. We became the focal point of the munitions industry and as a result Grantham was heavily raided by the Luftwaffe. As soon as they heard the roar of the planes overhead the townspeople would rush out of their houses and sleep in the ditches.

Meanwhile I was in charge of 2,000 women who made the bullets. I had my own office and felt quite a person, but without my secretary Miss Ellis I could never have done it. She was my backbone; stalwart and buxom, and always trying to convert me to Christian Science. It was particularly frightening on moonlit nights in winter snow when the factory silhouette could be seen clearly. I had to make quick decisions and the snow had to be cleared. Once we even attempted to make a mock factory with soot as a decoy for the Luftwaffe. In the end we built little subsidiaries around Grantham, and one is still in existence as a cow shed. As a last defence we actually mounted a gun on the office block and when we did shoot down a Junkers 88, Max Beaverbrook sent us its propeller as a trophy for our social hall. On cold nights I used to go round with a Ministry of Aviation bucket of rum to give to those manning the gun. We were very lucky that we never had a direct hit.

However, one day part of the factory was bombed and I had to make an announcement to all the factory women saying: 'Please stay calm and follow me'. I led them out the doors at the other end of the factory. We were terrified and praying for our lives but we managed to get out in time. I discovered I had some power in my hands to administer calm to the distressed, which I used on many occasions in the factory. Here is how my aunt Diana described the event in a letter to John Julius, on 5th February 1941: 'The other day in the big gun works in Grantham where Ursula works, a bomb exploded and another one fell, unexploded, in a workshop. They sent for the bomb disposal expert and your old friend, poor Perry Brownlow, had to take him to inspect the bomb. Perry's knees were shaking and his teeth chattering like castanets, while the expert knelt down with a stethoscope and applied it to the bomb's lungs. He then got up and said he would like to go and think about it for half an hour … he went back and deftly removed the pin and the detonator, boiling hot, which he placed in Perry's hands. He could scarcely hold them. The expert said every bomb is different and needs careful thought and diagnosis before dealing with it, like a human patient.'

There was nothing I didn't know about those women. Drink wasn't allowed in the factory but they would always find ways to smuggle it in. Sometimes they would mix alcohol with ink and bring it in an inkwell. It took me a long time to discover that trick. Others would try to find an excuse to be laid off ill because it was very dangerous work, although it didn't require a high degree of skill. They worked on chronometric machines with nine rotating steel rods and had to have their heads very close which meant their hair could get caught.

We worked long hours into the night and sometimes I went home in the dark in my cart. It was a proper gig with two huge yellow wheels and a black body, very chic. I bought the whole equipage from a drunken merchant in Grantham for £100. Sunny Titchfield, heir to the Portland estate and a great friend of my mother, used to come and stay with us. Sunny gave me the most beautiful whip to use, plaited leather, ivory and silver tipped with the Portland crest, which had belonged to his mother

Winnie, Duchess of Portland. It was very long but light, and handled wonderfully and I still have it today. I drove the eight miles home in the pitch black. You had to be brave because everybody was doing abnormal things during the war. This lovely gig had beautiful lights on the sides but because of the blackout they were covered, so you only see a tiny amount of light, the size of a fingernail. The gig was drawn by a young chestnut filly with four white feet and she would know the way home by herself. I used to offer everybody lifts but nobody would accept as they were too terrified. I never let it gallop but we would trot so fast that at Denton village we used to go round the corner on one wheel.

At Grantham I used to leave the gig in the vet's yard near the factory and the railway line. The vet was terrified of my going under the railway bridge when the Flying Scotsman was thundering past, so used to insist on holding the bridle. When I got home, Mr Durrants, the groom who had taught my sister and me to ride at a very early age, would look after the filly for me. He had been a young coachman on the box of carriages in Hyde Park as a boy and knew all about curry combing and cleaning a horse that had been flat out for miles and was covered in sweat. 'You'll break this poor filly's wind if you go that fast', he would scold me, but he would bring it in perfect condition to the front door the next day.

I never could have managed without him. Many years later I was astonished when an unknown lady came up to me at a festivity my brother Charles was hosting on the lawns at Belvoir, saying: 'You saved my life. I shall never forget it!' She had worked in the TNT shed at the factory in Grantham with the high explosives during the war.

I used to keep bees with one of the gardener's wives. We would save the sack of sugar that the government gave to bee-keepers to sustain their bees in winter, taking the honey needed for the boys home on leave but leaving enough for the bees to sustain the hive in winter. You would get as much as fifty to one hundred pounds of honey per hive. I loved the bees and the only time I was really stung was when I was invited to go to London for VJ Day and so could not go. I was furious to miss out but was in agony with my legs as swollen as bolsters. At least it immunised me for life against bee stings.

Friendships forged in times of crisis have a special quality. At the factory I got to know Gwen Collier, who had been Denis Kendall's mistress and now became my best girlfriend. After the war she went back to nursing and became the matron of a big hospital in America. My other close friend was my cousin Liz Hofmannsthal, who was my Aunt Marjorie Anglesey's second daughter. She married Raimund von Hofmannsthal, son of Hugo von

Hofmannsthal, a poet and the librettist of Richard Strauss. When they married they often visited Schloss Prielau in Zell am See in Austria, but they continued to live in London near Marble Arch. They were a very romantic pair and had two children, a boy and a girl. Raimund was very typically Austrian, very musical and slightly fat and relaxed, extremely entertaining after diner. He was a great friend of the Coopers. Liz and I were so close because we had come out together, were train-bearers and spent many country weekends together. She loved art like me but was very urban and stylish. I was more of a country girl and as my life gravitated more and more to hunting our friendship rather waned until we got older.

I didn't make girlfriends very easily as I didn't feel the need. I always enjoyed the quantity of men friends who flocked around me, but I remained bonded like a twin with my sister Isabel. I wrote to Isabel on crested Belvoir Castle paper edged in black, as we were still in mourning for my Father.

> *'My darling Bella*
> *Sunday 7th May 1940*
> *Thank you for your beautiful letter and many thanks for the lovely photographs. Forgive me for not answering it before, but I have cut my finger quite badly on my right hand cleaning a*

looking glass for the new house – it is only this morning that I have had the stitches out.

The weekend here was quite fun. Charles and John came plus Gena; Henry and Mary came over from Thorpe for dinner and it was all quite gay, forget the war touch.

I had a pathetic letter from Diana Valish from Portugal. She, Lulu, the children and Pa and Ma Esmond are on their way to America, poor things, having lost everything. God, how I feel for them, don't you?

…….. At the moment we have three hundred soldiers in the stables and houses round. They arrived at nine o'clock one night without letting anyone know of their arrival – you can imagine what a rush this was. Sad to say we cannot get into our house till Sept as it is almost impossible to get labour for such things nowadays... Darling, I am sending you little shoes for the baby and a toy.

How is Loel? I do think they have done him a dirty deed in sending him to York without the DFC or promotion of any kind. I think of you up there, poor sweet, but still you have your husband which is a lot these days. Mother is well and I think as happy as possible. We have red warnings all the time here, even more than Grantham or London. I find most of the people here are a bit frightened, especially at night – I can't help laughing, I am sure I don't know why, but everyone looks so odd at night, with all the different night preparations! …..

I long to see you, but when? The house has a lot more boxes in it, you can guess what they are!

My hand hurts me quite a lot so I must end this terrible letter. All my love to you and Loel.

Ursula'.

Once you get into a rut you can't get out of it, and the war was a rut! I got into the rut of permanently thinking about safety and the preservation of me and everybody. I was always on the lookout which served me well towards the end of the war, because you never heard the doodlebugs until it was too late. One night I had to leap out of a taxi outside John Lewis in London and ended up in a gutter with the driver lying on top of me. Every time I go shopping there I remember that.

The railway station at Grantham, which was the first stop of the Flying Scotsman, had been put in such a stupid place that all the German bombers had to do was to fly straight up the railway line. They had huge targets to destroy in Coventry and the Midlands, and Belvoir Castle on its hill was one of their landmarks en route. On their return they would jettison their unused bombs over Belvoir Vale.

In London you went out to dinner with your tin hat because nobody knew what would happen, and even Buckingham Palace was bombed. Every night in bed I couldn't sleep but I knew unshakeably that we would win. It was only when the Japanese came into the war that my heart sank. I thought this was an escalation to put the stopper on the bottle. Everybody drank a lot, laughed a lot and loved each other when you thought you could be dead in five minutes. It was as if you were constantly drunk because you couldn't bear to think about it.

People told me I was beautiful but I never thought so. I always thought my sister was prettier, with the most ebullient personality which lit up a room. All my brothers' friends flocked to her when they were on leave – Max Aitken, Seymour Berry, Ivor Wimborne, Robert Cranborne, Anthony Head, Bob Laycroft and goodness knows how many more. So many of them became famous in the world. Seymour Berry was a boyfriend of mine and the 2nd Viscount Camrose, the son of Lord Camrose, who owned the *Daily Telegraph*. He was a journalist who became an MP, very handsome and dashing, and I was very keen on him. He never flew but was always around in that milieu as he was Loel's best friend. Many years later at the age of seventy-five he would marry The Hon. Joan Yarde-Buller, Loel Guinness' first wife. Ivor Guest, 2nd Viscount Wimborne, who also became an MP, was an inveterate lady-killer. He came from great wealth and his family owned Wimborne house in Arlington Street which is now part of the Ritz Hotel. His father, Lord Wimborne, was a cousin of Winston Churchill and formerly Lord Lieutenant of Ireland, as well as being a great friend of Perry Brownlow and the dreaded Wallis Simpson.

Robert Cranborne, the 5th Marquess of Salisbury, was a great friend of my brothers and forever coming to stay at Belvoir. From Hatfield House, the family seat, he was heir to an unparalleled political tradition as his grandfather was Robert Gascoyne Cecil, the Prime Minister. His family owned the Salisbury Estates which encompassed a large part of London. Salisbury became Secretary of State of the Colonies and served under Churchill, Anthony Eden, and Harold Macmillan.

Anthony Head and Bob Laycroft took it in turns to be besotted about me but I just wasn't interested. Nevertheless whenever I had leave I would go and stay with Isabel and Loel where one met the world where we all, after the ticker-tape of war, were drinking away our sorrows.

Chapter Six
Flying High

Just before the war very rich people who loved flying had started buying these little airplanes called Hurricanes. Lady Stanley had a big house near Biggin Hill where they would all go for flying weekends with the most wonderful hospitality: Loel Guinness, Max Aitken, and Roger Bushell. Portia Stanley was married to one of my mother's best friends. When war was declared she invited all the young men about town and their wives and girlfriends to come and stay. When they weren't flying they would go out at night with a revolver and a torch to shoot grey squirrels in a sort of mad, drunken way to take their minds off the horrors. They were in such an important position in the war because they knew how to fly. By the time the war really took hold and we all lived in an atmosphere of constant dread, the women were no longer invited as it was thought too wild for them.

Tragically nearly all of them were killed. Loel Guinness, who married my sister and I liked very much, was in charge of 601 squadron. Max Aitken was Lord Beaverbrook's son, small and energetic and a great character. He was a superb shot and on raids never failed to shoot down two or three planes, just like high pheasants. Roger Bushell was older than the rest, a brilliant lawyer. All these men had come to my coming out ball at Belvoir. Until then I always used to say that if Hitler had wanted to walk down the Mall instead of the Champs-Elysées there was nothing to stop him. To think of these few brilliant men in aeroplanes with nothing over their heads against great clouds of bombers, like a flock of starlings, so many you couldn't count them. How they ever contemplated tackling the Germans I never knew, because they were in their forties and didn't have the fearlessness of youth.

It was on one of these flying weekends when I met my first husband, Anthony Marreco. He was amazingly handsome in his Fleet Air Arm uniform and brilliantly clever, conceited and sure of himself. He was a barrister and had also studied at RADA because he wanted to deliver speeches in court with perfect resonance. He was full of fun and very progressive, unlike anyone I had ever met before. He made a beeline for me and pursued me relentlessly, threatening to commit suicide if I didn't marry him.

Ursula and her sister Isabel in the 17th century silver punch bowl at Belvoir Castle. The bowl was bought in 1682 for £616.10s and weighs 1,979 oz.

Belvoir Castle today, but timeless.

Ursula on the terrace at Belvoir Castle in 1927.

Ursula outside the Lodge at Belvoir Castle for a meet of the Belvoir Hunt.

Ursula, her sister Isabel, and brother Charles, by Charles Edmund Brock (1870-1938).

Letter from Rex Whistler to Ursula and Isabel written as a rebus.

Envelope of letter from Rex Whistler to Ursula and her sister with stamps pasted over the tree tubs and envelope of letter from Rex Whistler to Ursula in 1927 with a picture of her finishing school at the Villa Malatesta, Via Foscolo, Florence.

Letter from Rex Whistler to Ursula with her Pekinese, Winky, in peer's robes and coronet.

Christmas card from Rex Whistler to Ursula.

Portrait of Ursula's father, 9th Duke of Rutland (1886-1940), in 1936 in the library at Belvoir Castle, by Etienne Drion (1885-1961).

Photograph of Ursula aged twenty-one, taken by Cecil Beaton with
only a brownie camera yet a masterpiece of light. She gave this signed
copy to her lady's maid with the inscription "To dear Jessie with many
thanks from Ursula Manners, 1939". Jessie's granddaughter returned it to
Belvoir Castle many years later.

Ursula with King George VI, Queen Elizabeth, Princess Elizabeth, and Princess Margaret, on the Buckingham Palace balcony in 1937 after the Coronation.

Ursula as Lady in Waiting at the Coronation, dressed by Norman Hartnell, photographed at Belvoir Castle as there was not one of her at Buckingham Palace, other than on the balcony.

Ursula and her sister Isabel at Haddon Hall, Derbyshire, after its restoration by their father, the 9th Duke of Rutland, with help from Ursula. He commissioned the painting of Haddon over the chimneypiece from Rex Whistler.

Haddon Hall today.

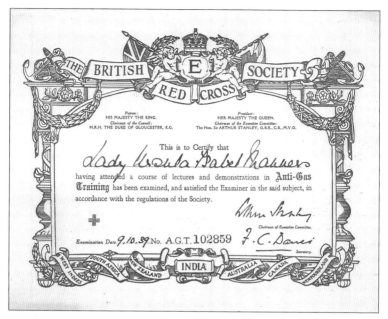

Ursula's British Red Cross Society Certificate of Anti-Gas Training in October 1939.

West Wratting Park, Cambridgeshire, built circa 1730 with late 18th century wings; Ursula's home from 1951.

Christening in 1953 at West Wratting Park of Ursula and Robert Erland d'Abo's son, John Henry Erland. Left to right: Robin d'Abo, Dowager Duchess of Rutland, Erland d'Abo, Lady Ursula d'Abo, Henry d'Abo, Francis Egerton, Nanny Neave, Sascha Phillips, Nicky Phillips, Gina Phillips, Andrew Scott, Billy Guinness, Roger Manners, Bunny Phillips, Lady Isabel Guinness, Duke of Rutland, Duchess of Northumberland.

TWO SHILLINGS
Volume CCXIX. No. 1834

The
TATLER
& BYSTANDER

MAR. 21
1956

Lady Ursula D'Abo and her two children

LADY URSULA D'ABO is the elder sister of the Duke of Rutland. In 1951 she married Mr. Erland d'Abo and this delightful picture shows her with their two children, Henry, who was born in 1953, and his sister Louisa who is two years younger. In the drawing room of their home, West Wratting Park, Cambridge. Lady Ursula's brother, who is the tenth Duke of Rutland, possesses two of the finest country houses in England, Haddon Hall, near Derby, and Belvoir Castle. He succeeded his father to the title in 1940.

Ursula with her son Henry and daughter Louisa Jane, photographed at West Wratting Park by *The Tatler* in 1956.

Ursula's daughter, Louisa Jane, painted by John Ward as the sole bridesmaid at the wedding in St Margaret's Westminster of the 5th Marquess of Dufferin and Ava to Serena (Lindy) Guinness in 1964.

Ursula at dinner with Paul Getty at his celebrated Tudor mansion, Sutton Place, Surrey, which was her base for five years until his death in 1976.

The enormous Villa at Palo Laziale on the sea-coast about 25 miles from Rome, bought by Paul Getty in 1960. It was built in 1640 by the Orsini family and is now an hotel.

Ursula at home in her Kensington flat in 1997.

Isabel and Ursula at Arthingworth circa 2008.

We used to escape to Scotland whenever we could and on one very special day high up in the hills above Edinburgh he proposed to me. We got engaged, much to the horror of my sister and Loel who did not like him, although he got on very well with my uncle Duff Cooper. He would stay with us at the Lodge when on leave and when my mother found out he didn't have a penny to his name she said: 'Darling, I don't mind, but do be aware I haven't any money to give you so you will have to live on love and fresh air'. He was very spoilt, an only child from a very sweet Cornish family.

I was fascinated by him and wanted to get married and have children, as I had seen how happy my sister was. When he came home he was the toast of the town, but Mother was rightly worried as I was only twenty and quite young for my age. I had been brought up in the tail end of the Victorian era, not even allowed to read books with love stories. He was very literary and used to spout acres of wonderful poetry. I shared his love for the arts and felt very sensually aroused by him in all senses.

We married on 25th July 1943 in the lovely small chapel at Belvoir Castle and had our honeymoon at Haddon Hall. I wore a very pretty white silk and net dress from Worth with a long veil. The ceremony was conducted by the vicar of our local church who was a family friend and had a grace-and-favour cottage on the estate. In the middle of the service he arranged a chair for me to sit on. He must have thought I was having a baby because it was all so hurried. I was furious at the presumption.

Within two days a naval car appeared to recall Anthony to duty and send him to the Far East on a small aircraft carrier. I never saw him and had no communication with him until the end of the war. When he came back he was a stranger and I didn't love him anymore. He was very distressed and fought against separating but in the end we divorced in 1948 which made me very sad. He said he wouldn't divorce me unless I returned the letters he had written to me, saying he would kill himself if I didn't marry him. He went on to have a very successful career in the law, working as a junior counsel in the Nuremberg war crimes trial, marrying twice more and surrounded by many lovely ladies who were obsessed by him. Mine was not the only wartime marriage which came to a bitter end. Against the backdrop of Armageddon so many short, intense romances blossomed which didn't withstand the drab realities of peace.

Chapter Seven
Escape to India

In 1946, after the war and a broken marriage, I was at a loose end, feeling lost and disoriented, when I ran into the Maharajah of Jaipur. I had first met Jai at a Court ball when I was barely seventeen. He was best friends with Pandit Nehru, the first Prime Minister of India, and a fantastic polo player who used to play frequently in England and go to all the parties. At Buckingham Palace he was dressed in an Afghan safa with a turban covered in the most dazzling jewels you could ever imagine to see. I was totally mesmerised by the jewels and his looks, because he was breathtakingly handsome. He had no wife in tow and was very young and never left my side. We didn't dance, we just sat and talked and had supper and left in the most beautiful Rolls Royce driven by a chauffeur who had a 'slung' jacket. I had never seen that uniform before. It was quite a long trip home from Buckingham Palace to Avenue Road in the north of London where the Rutlands had a leased house, and the conversation never ceased.

I never clapped eyes on him again until after the war. I looked like a scarecrow because I was extremely emaciated with rationing and work and he barely recognised me. He said, 'You must come to Jaipur to have some good food and sunshine'. I said I would love to. I met one of my sister's friends, Sir Robert Throckmorton, Bart. who was an Indophile. In conversation I talked about my acquaintance with Jai and the possibility of going to India. He encouraged me and said I must go. Eventually I found a plane carrying propellers to Delhi with a very competent pilot who agreed to take me as a passenger. It was a smallish aeroplane with a propeller and a fixed undercarriage and we had to stop every other minute to get fuel. We stopped for refuelling at Basra and Bahrain with no upheavals, and then flew to Baghdad where I bought carpets and one or two other things. I was at large and wanted rugs for home so went to the souk to have a look. After some tentative haggling I said to the salesman: 'I'll have those three.'

He was delighted and insisted on sending me back to the Sinbad Hotel followed by three little boys, each carrying a huge rolled rug on their heads. I sat in the foyer, wilting from the heat, and waited for the concierge to show me to my room. The beauty of the polished wood of the bar struck me, and that of the Arab men even more so. They were miles high and immensely handsome and arrogant. I paid my little boys and put my rugs in my room and collapsed.

The next morning we set off to Sharjah in the Persian Gulf, not far from Dubai. My crew were typically British, not revealing to me, thank God, their concerns about the state of the plane. Sharjah was manned by senior RAF officers in an airfield surrounded by barbed wire, who were protecting the jetty for flying boats to refuel on their way on their regular route to the Far East. It was burning hot and the airfield was just sand, vaguely pegged out. I was sitting and waiting for them to refuel the plane when the Captain of the fort said: 'You had better come and see Dubai with my organisation while you wait'. We set off with three motor cars, one in front, one behind and me in the middle, driving miles into the sand by compass. He told me: 'If we leave the car when we get out to walk, the villagers will dissect it. The car will be guarded by four men and we will take another four with us, because I don't dare take a white woman into the desert without protection'. Never had a white woman been in Dubai, and nor had many Western men.

He showed me a little harbour with the dhows, lovely steps down to the sea and huge baskets overflowing with oysters. The whole economy was based on pearls at that time but BP had just got permission to look for oil. He walked me through the village although everyone was very apprehensive. There was perfect sunshine, not too hot, which soothed my ruffled nerves. I never dreamed that the little seaport of Dubai would one day become a skyscraper town of immense wealth.

The aeroplane eventually took off with all the officers in the camp waving us good bye. 'Good luck over the shark-infested seas!' they said. Well my goodness, one engine caught fire just before we got to the sea and the pilot had to turn around, feathering the other engine, and we only just made it back to Sharjah. They didn't have any spares for the old plane. They tried to mend it but it was impossible.

Meanwhile I was expected in Delhi but there was no way to contact my host. I unrolled my rugs and lay in the sun with my hunting boots by my side and waited. I could feel the sun searing my skin and thought about my grandmother, who had always told me to cover my skin in the sun and lived in a world where hats had veils. I never took her advice, later to my deep regret.

Eventually a French aeroplane came in on its way to Saigon. I listened to the conversation of the crew and realised they were carrying bombs and bringing back wounded. The captain was young, handsome and charming: just what the doctor ordered in a situation of gloom. He said, 'We will give you a lift to Delhi and if you like you can see Saigon at the French government's expense, and then we will drop you in Delhi on the way back'. To make room for me on the plane they started to move aside bombs and lower a revolting stretcher covered in dried blood, but they found some champagne and chocolate for me. I told them I couldn't possibly have any champagne since I would get wildly drunk with the heat and because I was so tired. I only wish they were still alive today to thank them for their kindness. I would have loved to have visited Saigon, but by now was desperate to get to India.

When they dropped me in Delhi there was no Jai, until I realised we were at the military airport rather than the civilian one. Luckily Jai had the gumption to go and see if I was at the military airport and did find me eventually. He never usually got cross but was rather annoyed because he had been waiting for me for hours. He whisked me off in his private plane. 'Now you must change and be ready to have a welcoming meal', he greeted me. 'Twenty people are coming for lunch!' I had to try and look respectable even though there was no mirror to be found.

After the lunch in Jaipur I was shown to a beautiful huge room in the Rambagh Palace where

I stayed for many weeks, lapping up the delicious food, sunshine, laughter, and no sign of the war. The order of the day was breakfast in one's room, then tennis and the famous polo would take place just after lunch. The whole town went to watch and it was extraordinarily brilliant. The spectators were nearly all Indian men and were kept behind grilles, like a prison wall. I used to say if you took the grilles away they would still sit there clapping and screaming, not budging over the board which surrounded the playing field.

The Argentines were famous for breeding polo ponies, and while I was there a charming couple came to sell one hundred ponies. The husband was from one of the biggest old Argentine families and had a very beautiful young wife. While the husband was playing polo with Jai he fell and was kicked in the stomach by one of the ponies. They stretchered him off the field immediately and a doctor tried to help but could not staunch the internal haemorrhaging. He died right there in front of us. His wife was in a fearful state as they had not been married for long. I put my hands on her neck to soothe her and was able to relax her completely and calm the hysteria. The healing powers I had used in the factory were still there.

It was like going back to mediaeval times. The sentries on the gates were elephants, like we have guards for our Queen. Jai was virtually King of Rajasthan, the largest state of India and almost as big in area as Germany. (Now it is famous for the discovery of oil in Mangala in the north-west by the Scottish exploration company Cairn Energy, who bought the drilling rights from Shell. It has an extensive field of oil which has yet to be developed). I rode every day and had lovely massages. There was a constant stream of distinguished house guests such as Frank Whittle, who invented the jet engine, lots of English and foreign politicians, as well as Indian leaders like Pandit Nehru, and many others. People from all over the world came to see Jai who was much loved and seemed to know everyone. I particularly treasured my friendship with Nehru and enjoyed evenings in his company listening to the sacred Hindu poet Rabindranath Tagore. We kept in touch and exchanged letters over the years. He wrote to me on 3rd June 1949:

Prime Minister, India

Dear Ursula Manners,

Thank you for your note. I am glad you spent a few more hours in Kashmir. Of course you can keep the Ajanta books as long as you like and return them when it suits. The proper way to return them was to bring them yourself, but one must not expect too much?

I am returning your book and adding another, a recent publication. This is just a collection of odd writings and speeches on Gandhi.

I would love to visit Haddon Hall and perhaps I may do so one day. But I am a prisoner of fate and circumstance, more so than I have ever been before, and I do not know when I may go and what I might do. I have given up planning for the future so far as I am concerned. That has its advantages as well as its disadvantages.

All good wishes.
Yours ever
Jawaharlal Nehru

He wrote again on 22nd September saying

Dear Ursula,

…………….. I live a fevered existence, trying hard to keep pace with time and always failing. Why I do so is more than I can understand, when the beauty of this world beckons to me. But then the horror and the mess of this world call back. Perhaps it is just conceit to imagine that one can make any difference. Anyway this keeps me from the pleasures of yachting or

mountain climbing or even reading and writing. Certainly I get a certain excitement but the price one pays is heavy.

Yes I am passing through London on my way to America. I am likely to be there just a half day and then I shall be swallowed up in a whirl of rather frightening activities in the U.S.

Yours ....

The town of Jaipur was glorious. All the buildings were painted pale pink and the City Palace was romantically grand and guarded by elephants. Jai had three wives, two of whom lived in purdah in the palace. They were rarely seen but occasionally emerged to watch a polo tournament, where they would sit inside a Rolls Royce with black windows while a eunuch brought them food.

Every year there was an incredible celebration for the Festival of Colours which lasted for three days and was like the Arabian Nights. Every day was a different colour and the whole city dressed in that colour. There was a procession from the City Palace consisting of elephants decked in the colour of the day, led by a mahout holding a wondrous 18th century gold cornucopia at least two feet high. It was totally magical because of the smell of the steady stream of burping smoke coming from the elephants as they walked into the gloaming of the setting sun. The mahout heralded the procession and led the Goddess, dressed in rare jewels and sitting on a howdah throne on an elephant. Meanwhile there would be many elephants going by, all decorated in the same wondrous colour, and followed by a procession of animals: tigers, camels and black bears trotting along the streets. This happened every day for three days with every man, woman and child dressed in the colour of the day and I was transfixed. The last day was green, the colour of hope. As the sun set I was obsessed by the wonder of these processions.

Jai flew me around in his Dakota to see Bundi, Udaipur and the Taj, which shook my timbers for wonder. Everybody in England was so horrid, saying I was having a roaring affair with an Indian prince, but that was not the case. He was a generous host and treated me like a queen. He called me 'the Duchess'. He was always charming to me and remained a friend all my life. Wherever we would land on our expeditions there would be people on the side of the roads cheering. There was no communication but somehow they knew by human telegraph what was going to happen and they would close the roads that crossed his path. Jai was adored by the people who called him Kumanganay and clasped their hands and bowed as he passed.

The next time I went to Jaipur he was married to Ayesha, a daughter of the Maharajah of Cooch

Behar, a state in the north, near the Himalayas. She had been educated in England and Paris and was a great beauty. He took her everywhere and she was not in purdah. We had dances and she was a brilliant tennis player. She used to come to England when she was the widowed Queen Mother. She entered Indian politics in Delhi. At one stage she got more votes than Mrs Gandhi. However, her political career ended in disaster and there was a terrible period when she was put in prison by Mrs Gandhi. She was terrified of crowds and Indian prisons were very crowded, but all her friends rallied round. I used to go and have lunch with her regularly when she was back in England. Jai died tragically quite young from a polo fall in Cirencester in 1970. Ayesha died in Jaipur in 2010. She fell very ill in England and was flown back to India in a private ambulance plane, dying in Jaipur and was burnt in a funeral pyre in the Hindu fashion.

When I first went back to England I talked to everyone about how I had fallen in love with India. Bobby Throckmorton said he was off to shoot tigers. I needed no convincing to go again myself. I flew to Jaipur with Bobby in his Dakota and he took us to Cooch Behar for the shoot, Jai accompanying us to his brother-in-law's. What an extraordinary, memorable sight it was. There must have been twenty or more elephants and dozens of beaters and keepers passing through the beautiful jungle, with orchids everywhere. The elephant grass was rightly named because it was taller than the elephants. We would assemble in the morning with dew still on the grass and clamber onto our elephants' backs and lie on pads, feeling the very slow, rhythmic trundle of the huge beasts. The person in charge was Ayesha's younger brother Baya who rode a tiny, female elephant bareback with just his toes behind her ears to guide her. Ayesha's older brother Indriajit used to drink like a fish and nobody could stop him, so they made him dummy bullets for his gun, just in case there was a mishap.

Baya Cooch Behar would lead a long row of us to a completely wild bit of jungle, walking slowly up to a tree which the elephant would fell with sheer strength, uprooting the trunk, and walk over. Thus a ride was cleared for the guns to stand, with the elephant grass tickling our knees. I got onto Jai's elephant with our guns, and there was a string of guests and family on elephants with howdahs, with servants or friends behind them handing them the loaded guns. Someone shot the tiger and wounded it and blew the whistle for all the guns and beaters to make a vast circle around the wounded beast. The elephants closed in, trumpeting so loudly that noise filled the jungle. Then Baya on his tiny elephant opened the circle and shot the wounded tiger dead.

Sudden silence. After all the waiting, and nervous tension, the dramatic release was extraordinary.

I have never experienced anything so romantic as sauntering home in the gloaming with the heavy elephants' feet tramping incongruously on the sensitive plants which looked like water rippling, the jungle illuminated by fireflies. I asked the beaters if there was anything that bothers the elephant and they told me that sometimes a tiger would jump them but the thing that sent them into a frenzy was bees. Swarms would descend and sting them on their sensitive pale pink chops under their trunk, and under their tails. By the time the sun goes down it gets dark very quickly. We saw columns of smoke in the distance on the other side of the river where they were cooking piles of very big hot chapattis for the elephants. On the way we saw masses of sheep being looked after by shepherds who played the flute to them like in classical Greece: Et in Arcadio Ego.

It was all truly magical and I was so pleased that Bobby had made me go back. I stayed at the camp for a week and was given a baby leopard to look after. It was old enough to be separated from its mother and used to stroke my arm. The natives used to come and look at me as if I was a witch because leopards don't have pads but retractable claws. It became quite tame under my jurisdiction and I longed to bring it back to England but Jai refused to have it in the plane.

111

I was a very keen farmer by then and wanted to bring back Indian cattle to cross with an English cow. I went to stay with Elmhirst, the British Consul who had a dairy farm not far from Delhi. I was determined to go to an agricultural show by myself. Elmhirst thought I was mad, as four white women travelling in a train had recently been murdered. I thought I would be safer in a men only coach. There were four bunks: the man opposite was doped, the man above me was a nice Sikh. The train stopped at most stations and there was a nozzle with Jeyes fluid which came in and was vigorously sprayed. At a larger station they offered food, and the Sikh above me said: 'Would you like me to get you a dessicana?' This turned out to be a round tray with little pots of different and delicious curries, and it left me with a life long passion for spicy food. At the show I saw a magnificent pair of buffaloes, their oil-massaged skin shining in the sun and white-tipped tails. I thought they would be ideal for the estate at home, and I am sure if I had had enough money or spoken the local dialect I would have tried to bring them home.

Before I left Rajasthan for the last time, Ayesha gave me lots of beautiful saris and I brought back a wedding dress which is now on show at Belvoir Castle. In Rajasthan the sacred birds are peacocks and pigeons. If you shoot either you go to prison. The peacock appears as the crest of the flag of Rajputana and is also the Rutland crest, which seemed a happy coincidence. They kept one old boy to do nothing but keep the pigeons off the roof of the palace. That's all he did all day, throw a tennis ball on a string to stop them landing. They couldn't shoot them, you see. It was like a picture in a book. They did serve European food at banquets but I liked hot food, mangoes and papayas. Everything was done on such a vast scale which was natural to them because of the land, the rivers, the mountains. There were very few roads so we flew everywhere.

Everything was primitive: the skirts which the local women wore were very full-skirted of dark red wool with a black line in it. They would lay them out on the stone and pleated them with their fingers to dry in the sun, the way it had been done for centuries. It was the main uniform of the women, just as the sari is for the rest of the country. I felt like an ambassadress and was one of the first women to fly by herself.

Chapter Eight
The Accident

After the war I had to reorient my life completely because my work in the factory had ceased and my marriage to Tony Marecco was over. I felt rather lost and didn't know what to do or where to live. I went to London and a good friend, one of my sister's circle called Anthony Nutting who had become an MP, said 'Why not take my flat? It's cheap and fairly central'. So he let me have his London pied-à-terre in the Edgware Road for very little money. I made it my home and started hunting around for a job and for somebody to help me in the flat.

I tracked down one of my wartime Grantham factory workers, an oldish woman who lived near Belvoir, and asked if would she like to work for me. I was delighted when she agreed and, although we both had to adapt because it was a small flat, we became great friends. She was known as the

Gorgon by my men friends. I think I created a lot of jealousy at that time and didn't realise until I was older why men were attracted to me. I should have chummed up with more women. One of my cousin's husbands actually jumped onto the roof of a car and banged on the bedroom window of my flat. Luckily the Gorgon saw him off. In the end she left me to become my brother's housekeeper at Belvoir and I was disappointed, feeling she had abandoned me just at the wrong time.

Off I went to see old Sir William Root, an acquaintance who ran a shop selling motorcars in Piccadilly opposite the Ritz. Despite not knowing the first thing about cars I managed to persuade him to give me a job on the showroom floor. I didn't do too badly as all my friends dropped by and took me out to lunch. Every other weekend I would spend with my sister Isabel, setting off on Friday afternoon on the train bumbling down to Portsmouth where she and Loel kept their yacht. Loel was in some kind of job which necessitated him being in London. It was a steam yacht and the stoker had to stoke away constantly, and quite small, just big enough for a couple and me. It was such fun being out at sea and sometimes when the weather was good enough we would go as far as Deauville.

At this time I was being courted by two lovely boys, Erland d'Abo and Johnnie Dalkeith, heir to the

Duke of Buccleuch. I tried to keep them separate but I think they guessed about each other. I fell madly in love with Erland but knew he was a lady-killer. I was never sure he really loved me until one night which changed my life forever. We were driving to his estate at West Wratting, near Cambridge. It was a miserable night, pelting with rain, and Erland was not in a good mood. I discovered later he had just said goodbye to one of his mistresses. She was married. He said he was not sure he really loved me and I was very distressed. As we were driving along fate took a terrible turn. A parked sand lorry with no lights, on our side of the road, loomed up in front. With oncoming cars on the other side of the road there was no escape and we ploughed bang into the truck. We were going fast but, thank God, in a Bentley, which acted as a buffer. Erland was saved by the steering wheel. I was sitting in a bucket seat, which was lucky for me because there were no seat belts, but my head was slammed onto the dashboard. My nose was pushed into my skull by the serrated knob of the windscreen wiper.

I was not unconscious and could feel no pain, but my face was pouring with blood and I thought I was blind. When the policeman arrived I asked him to lift up the piece of skin over my eye and realised I could see. They took me off to Letchworth Cottage Hospital. I was in despair and screaming to see the famous plastic surgeon Archibald McIndoe, who had done miraculous work with wounded soldiers. The nurses told me that he wasn't there but by the luck of the draw there was a plastic surgeon called Rainsford Mowlem, of even greater eminence. He didn't like publicity but he had done amazing work with war casualties, and all the doctors themselves would go to him themselves. He took one look at me and said, 'Put her in an ambulance and take her straight to the London Clinic and when I have finished here I will operate on her myself'. Speed is essential and he knew it.

He was temperamental and shouted at every one but his skill was universally respected. He did the most wonderful job on me. He was furious at what had happened and wrote to Bentley saying they should not have a corrugated knob of that nature on a dashboard. In fact the knob had pierced the thickest part of my frontal skull which had protected the eye. They took me out of the ambulance into the London Clinic in Harley Street and I was whisked straight into surgery. That is the secret with plastic surgery – you need to act instantly. Because he was so well known there were no modern preliminaries like forms to be filled in. One just went straight to the operating theatre. He only did dire cases, no beautification work at all. From the moment he said: 'Take her to the London Clinic', I knew I was going to be all right. Mr Mowlem had an assistant called Miss Clayton, who was a wonder. They made the perfect team because she could control his erratic temperament. I lay back knowing I would still have a face after all. After the operation he told me he wished he had taken a photograph of my face beforehand to compare with the result.

I was so impressed by his skill that later on I asked if I could watch him operate and he agreed, so long as the patient didn't mind. The poor man, a soldier, had had one side of his face blown up. Mr Mowlem took a chisel to the hip bone like a carpenter, cutting very thin slices of bone which he put in a bowl with water. When he added the penicillin powder it looked like raspberries and cream. Then he applied the bone, moulding his face with his thumbs, standing back and walking away like an artist sculpting a portrait bust.

I started to heal but there was still a great hollow on my forehead and Miss Clayton said: 'You can't let her go home like that!' Eventually I had to have three operations with a year's interval between each, because bone takes such a long time to heal. When the operation is finished you see how it will look at the end, but then it starts to swell and takes a year to subside. I cannot remember how long I was in the Clinic. Weeks went by in a daze. Before the car crash I had been going out with Johnnie Dalkeith,

who was just one year older than me. He was from
an eminent Scottish family with great estates and we
were all as happy as could be. His father, the Duke
of Buccleuch, passionately wanted Johnny to marry
me, and in fact the Duke was the only member of the
family who came to see me in the London Clinic.

The Buccleuchs were from the same world as
my family. His sister, a great friend of mine, nearly
married my brother Charles. Johnnie was charming,
and an MP by then, and needed the perfect wife. I
don't think he had met lots of girls as he had joined
the Navy when he was very young during the war and
served as an ordinary sailor on the Arctic Convoys,
through freezing ice for months on end. I didn't
really get to know him until after the war when I was
working in London. Everyone said I should meet
him and when my brother finally introduced me to
him he told me he had been chasing me. He knew all
my brothers and had a sister, Elizabeth, who married
the Duke of Northumberland. She was a delicious,
giggly, gregarious girl with immense charm and
sense of humour who proceeded to have five Percy
children. She remained one of my best friends until
her death in 2012.

Johnnie didn't come to London often and when
he did he lived in his parents' flat. Most of the time
he was running the huge family estates in Scotland. I
used to go and visit him when I could get away from

work. I will never forget my first visit. I took the night sleeper to Scotland, not knowing what I was in for, and the guard told me that the train would stop at Thornhill in Dumfriesshire especially to let me off. Apparently they would always stop at Thornhill for the Duke of Buccleuch and his guests. A car was waiting at the station to take me to the castle.

I never thought anything could be more beautiful than Drumlanrig Castle. This early morning arrival was never to be forgotten. A pale pink castle set in the middle of a country made especially beautiful by centuries of careful tree planting and set in nature's frame of hills, like a huge pink casket in the rising sun. It looked like a principality. It was the largest private estate in the country. At the top of many stone steps I found the Duke waiting for me, followed by footmen who carried my somewhat odd luggage, and a side-saddle to boot. I was led straight into a huge panelled dining room with windows showing onto a courtyard in perfect proportion to the room. Two outstandingly pretty gold coffee pots and milk pots fluted in gold stood on their own little stands on the long table, silhouetted in the glitter of a rising sun. I was accustomed to beautiful surroundings and things at home but this was almost too grand.

After that I was shown to my room by the perfect secretary, Miss McKechin, apologising that the flowers on the mantelpiece were less than perfect. It was as though we had known each other for years and I was already part of the house. Johnnie was never very demonstrative in his affections while his mother was staying because I was not considered suitable by her, and well do I remember being in great awe of her.

Johnnie's father was Walter Montagu-Douglas-Scott, 8th Duke of Buccleuch. He was a most charming gentleman, an MP and loved by all on his vast estates. He was Captain General of the Royal Company of Archers and was a Knight of the Order of the Thistle, of which he became Chancellor, the most ancient and highest honour in Scotland. Interestingly, when Walter died the Duchess wrote a long letter to me saying how much he had really liked me. We stayed in touch over the years and Johnnie wrote to me from Sandringham on 31st January 1950.

Dearest Ursy,

Thank you so much for your letter, wherein I cannot understand your accusation that I had not written to you! How terribly exciting for you to be off to India once more and with prospects of lots of other travels. South America sounds most intriguing – I really do admire the way in which you encompass the world, showing such initiative and enterprise – all the more remarkable from what I have seen of you in foreign travels.

You have chosen a very good time to go away, as the penetrating curtain of cold descends over the country. It looks like we shall be icebound for weeks and weeks while you languish in saris on cool verandas amidst blazing heat.

Hunting certainly looks to be at a standstill for some time to come, so there will be no excuses for not doing some good hard work at home. Elizabeth and Hughie came to Bowhill for a weekend to hunt, but of course brought frost with them.

Bowhill is now most comfortable and liveable and piping hot – the only trouble being no servants.

I was sad not be able to be able to have a glimpse of you as I flashed through London last Tuesday, but as usual out of one train and into the next.

Peter Scott is here and has just given a most fascinating lecture with superb coloured cinema of his last Arctic exhibition to northern Canada – a most interesting man.

As you may well imagine your present abode is a source of justified sore feeling in this house and the dining table has shaken with wrath at the mention of the great loss.

Best of luck in your great adventures and happy happy times.
With love from
Johnnie

The weekend went terrifically well and we then proceeded to one of their other vast houses, Bowhill, south of Edinburgh. We were to go hunting there but they found it difficult to find a suitable animal for my side-saddle. My side-saddle was eventually mounted on a much quieter animal than I was used to, but worst of all she was unfit and absolutely incapable of keeping up with the hunt. She had no inclination of getting into a canter, thank goodness, as it would have been quite unsafe. Altogether I was not impressed with the Buccleuch hunt world. The horses were not fit because they simply had not been exercised enough before the season.

Left behind in unknown country, I decided to head back to Bowhill which I found rather intimidating. However I progressed very slowly and eventually caught up with a lady going home the same way who took pity on me, which was helpful as my Dobbin by that time was completely lame. Afterwards she kindly sent me a perfect little veil for a top hat as a gift.

I went back to London then went away the following week to stay with my boyfriend Erland.

That was what my life was like at that time. Everybody said I was after men. The truth was the other way around. I was still shy and, as a semi-Victorian child, I hardly knew where babies came from. I didn't know how to manage all these eager men. If I had it would have been more fun. My sister was the complete opposite. I always thought she was much prettier than me and went bang, bang, bang and married so young.

After the car accident Erland was distraught with guilt and had proposed to me in the car as I went into the Clinic. I said: 'You must wait a year until I know what I am going to look like'. The terrible smash on the road to West Wratting changed everything. Now I contemplated marrying the man who had driven me into the back of a truck. I did not think for a moment that it was his fault. He didn't drive badly and it was just one of those appalling accidents. He felt dreadfully guilty, especially as he himself had been protected by the steering wheel and had not been hurt.

I stuck to my word for twelve months and after a year's break I eventually agreed to marry Erland. He was itching to marry me straight away but my face still hadn't recovered from the surgery. The first party I went to was at Syon House where everybody surreptitiously stared at me, expecting the worst, but then were delighted I looked almost normal after the horror stories they had heard about the crash and my treatment. The whole family came to the wedding and we were married in the little village church of West Wratting on 22nd November 1951. We had to get special permission from the Church because Erland had been married before to Mary Graham-Clarke and had a little boy, Robin, who was at Prep School. I wore a white Norman Hartnell dress and had no bridesmaids, and Erland's brother was Best Man. Our wedding was a wonderful party and I was very happy. Then we went on our honeymoon which wasn't so hot, because he had selected a ghastly place in the Channel Islands and I was still in pain recovering from my head injury. It was an unfortunate choice of his secretary's. We soon headed home to a new life together and I was more and more in love with him every day.

Chapter Nine
West Wratting

We settled down to married life at a mellow brick 18th century country house in West Wratting, just fifteen miles south east of Cambridge. Erland was a friend of my middle brother Johnnie and ten years older than me, a successful stockbroker, divorced with a nine year old son. He had found West Wratting when he went to visit an old friend who lived in a village near Cambridge. The house was derelict and had been used as a school during the war. Erland knew the area well because he had been at Cambridge as an undergraduate. On that first visit in the pelting rain, standing with umbrellas under a fir tree near the house, he had decided to buy the place.

My husband went to London every day from Audley End station to Liverpool Street. The train took him almost to the door of his office at a stockbroking firm called Myers and our driver, Mr Chapman, would meet him at Audley End at the end of the day. I was exhausted but happy to find such a beautiful house in its infancy. Nothing within it was furnished except for one bedroom, the hall and a very basic kitchen, so it was a huge challenge to make it liveable. It had all the original period mouldings but no mod cons: no loos, no water, nothing, and all the cottages on the estate were derelict. During the war they put in a pipeline for water from Cambridge to the nearby aerodrome, but when that closed down after the war nothing was left in the house. We had to begin from scratch. It was the start of an exciting project, which I enjoyed more than anything because I had done it in the past with my father at Haddon.

Every day produced a new challenge, all of which was great fun in a way because it was one's own approach to everything, not an architect or designer, just my husband and me. It was a huge task but the beauty of the house was a constant inspiration. We took down the derelict staff wing, which was a hideous later addition to the house. We made a well-proportioned dining room by taking down the wall which divided the pantry and the servants hall. I only wished I had gone to town on a splendid mantelpiece. But I had no more money by that time as I had exhausted every penny tearing down the wing between the orangery and the house.

The terrace had a wonderful view over the garden and countryside, which made all the hard work worthwhile. I did my best with the garden but instead of standing back and looking at the project as a whole I just did it bit by bit when I found the energy. My family told me to plant trees because that part of the country is very bleak. I should have planted thousands of trees but I didn't then realise that in thirty years you can see the full effect of an avenue or wood. If only one could be more relaxed in life and let things just happen, sew seeds and let things grow. That way things do fall into place, but it's the hardest thing to do because you feel the passion and want to get on in a flurry, and never make the right decisions. We had no money but I believe money shouldn't come into everything. It certainly shouldn't be the prime factor in marriage. If you are truly in love and work together with intelligence to make a successful marriage you will reap the rewards with style and artistry. Money may follow. Magic entered my soul during these years when Erland and I were creating this wonderful house together for our future.

I had been brought up accustomed to village life and now we became truly involved in cricket on the green at the weekends. At West Wratting there was one dear old lady in the Post Office shop, who was the heart and soul of the village. You could buy anything you needed there and she also took classes for the little children. The shop was at the bottom of our drive in a charming house with a bell which rang when you opened the door. It was opposite a pub called The Chestnut, which didn't seem to have a very friendly atmosphere, perhaps because it wasn't owned by the person who ran it. Otherwise there were two other pubs and a church with a nice vicar. He came to see me one morning, when we were all working in the greenhouse, and was utterly charming and persuasive. He said he would love to have stayed if he could have collected some more souls. I should have bewitched him and promised to come to church on Sundays and help him collect souls, but I was so busy and tired I didn't always make it. His small flock was not enough to support him and he left.

Lots of the cottages still had thatched roofs. Years later when the shop closed – it was very sad because that lady represented the warmth and continuity of village life, which was dying throughout England. I always remember my mother building a lovely village hall in Rowsley, near Haddon. It comprised a reading room and a large hall where lots of local events could take place. Sadly with my husband working in the City and always wanting to save money to buy more land for farming, I wasn't able to follow in Mother's footsteps.

When the vicar left we didn't have anyone permanent and had to share a visiting vicar who covered about six villages. Looking back I was such a fool not to have encouraged him to stay as he might have been able to help me and the children in the future. It became very tiring for me, constantly taking them to football matches myself. I found two elderly maids called Robina and Rebecca who knew the ways of a big house. One had been a parlourmaid and one a housemaid and I was very spoiled by them as they brought me breakfast in bed. Friends who came to stay were impressed.

Farming seemed the answer, as we were in good East Anglian arable country. We started to invest in sturdy farming equipment. Erland made it his big thing to save every penny and buy more land so as to make it a viable proposition which would pay for itself, and with any luck a bit more. The existing dairy was already a paying concern but it was only tiny.

When Erland told me about his farm many years earlier, I thought: 'What can I give him as a wedding present? Something to do with West Wratting', because by this time he was wildly keen on the property. Firstly I thought about shooting because he loved that and adored going to Lady Delamere's shoot on the land around her house at Six Mile Bottom. She was Lady Mountbatten's sister and married to Lord Delamere who had survived the Happy Valley scandal in Kenya. She was a widow and adored my husband. Years ago Edward VIII would go and stay there as it was such a wonderful partridge shoot.

I decided to buy him a bull so he could start a proper beef herd. I solicited the help of my friend Lord Beaverbrook, who had recently brought over an excellent manager from New Zealand to run his estate. He said he would let me have the best one of that year, and suddenly I was the proud purchaser of a pedigree Aberdeen Angus bull. It arrived in state all the way from Scotland, proud and beautiful to look at, dark and glossy with manicured hooves. To my utter disbelief all it did was lie in the ditch and flap its eyelashes. It never performed once and never produced anything. It cost me nearly £1,000, which I barely had at the time. Nevertheless we pursued our farming and it became really very exciting.

Meanwhile I started gardening and searching for antiques to fill the house. When I was planning the landscaping off the terrace I visited several gardens in the area and found a house which had been burned out called Uffington near Stamford, which had a marvellous stone parquet floor on the terrace, which fitted together without any concrete. You could still glimpse it between the overgrown grass and the broken balustrades and fountains. It inspired me to pave the terrace at West Wratting but it took me a long time to find stones which had the right proportions. I solicited the help of an old nursery gardener who put me to shame with his encyclopaedic knowledge. He helped me plant a herbaceous border and to find magnificent magnolia bushes of the grandiflora variety, with gorgeous waxy petals and evergreen leaves coloured deep russet on the underside. He was very knowledgeable about striking from cuttings and found three absolute beauties about five foot high in Jersey. He arranged for them to be sent by boat and train and I went to fetch them at the station in Cambridge. The two on the terrace flourished but the third one I planted deep in the garden didn't make it. They grew fifty feet high and scented the rooms when the windows were open in summer. I have the prettiest photograph of my granddaughter Anouska sitting under a bloom when she was a little girl. Never did I imagine when I was planting those bushes that one day I would be ninety-five and have a granddaughter of twenty at university in America. My dear gardener sadly died before the garden was finished.

I was very friendly with an antiques dealer in Cambridge called Mr Beazor. He would lend me some lovely pieces if he found something which he thought would fit in my house. Having the chance to live with beautiful furniture helped me develop my style. When I first moved in I was fanatical about decorating on a budget. I used to paddle off to every known sale room and managed to find the most striking gold carved bits of wood, which would have normally gone on top of a pelmet, just loose in an old antiques shop. There were three pieces which gave me the idea of creating my own four poster bed. I found two mahogany poles with the help of a lady at Robert Sayle, the John Lewis shop in Cambridge. I had acquired an embroidered quilt which I wanted to be the focal point of my new guest bedroom. In Stamford I found some paintings of Naples harbour by an inferior artist, but quite charming. I wanted pink silk for the drapes on the bed but it was too expensive. As an alternative I bought cheaper percale cotton, which was shiny on the front but matt on the underside. We pleated the back and drew the inside of the canopy together in the middle of the room through a wooden hoop into a rose made of the same fabric. That was the first bedroom I did and it was thrilling. In the master bedroom I was even more ambitious and had a bedhead made with the initials of my family, and gophered frills on the drapes. This was a kind of smocking which you still see on children's dresses.

I'd never been so busy in my life. I was passionately determined to have a family, and being married to Erland was a joy because there I was, free as air. He longed to have children with me and yet in the beginning I didn't seem to get pregnant.

I was worried if it was due to problems from the car crash or if I was too old at nearly forty. Finally my doctor sent me to a female obstetrician and I had my fallopian tubes blown. I then proceeded to have children every minute. I was in the London Clinic on and off for seven years with continuing treatment for the accident, gall bladder problems and three babies. When I started a baby, oh dear me was I happy.

I was over the moon when I had a wonderful big bouncing boy weighing nine pounds on 8th October 1953 whom we called John Henry Erland. We left the London Clinic as happy as sandboys and drove straight to West Wratting. A friend of my mother had helped me make a lovely bedroom for Henry out of an awful wing which used to house the dog kennels. And we made a night nursery with French windows onto the garden out of a huge wood store. I had a vision of children running out onto the lawn from the nursery. The first letter of congratulations I got was from Mr Durrance, our groom at home, saying he hoped he'd got a good leg for a boot, meaning that he would be as good at riding and hunting as his mother. I remember fondly how my father made Mr Durrance promise he would look after Isabel and I when we went hunting, but he couldn't keep up with us and usually ended up at the pub, praying nothing would happen to us.

Running the house with a new baby was an experience, with very few servants after the war. A maternity nurse came back with me from the Clinic but stayed for only a few weeks, so I hired an old fashioned nanny with grey hair. I needed someone to manage the kitchen and was lucky enough to hear that Mrs Anderson, my mother's old retired cook, was available because the sister with whom she was going to live in Troon in Scotland had died. She agreed to come because she always loved me, and she was quite unique. She had somebody to help in the kitchen because she was by that time very old, but she planned the menus and bought the food and did all the cooking. I couldn't wait for her arrival and once she did I never had to think about it at all. My word did she do it economically. It was very difficult to find somebody to work with her in the kitchen because she was accustomed to so many maids doing all the washing up. At first I couldn't find anyone but eventually found a man who had been in some delinquent home or prison. He seemed to be fairly normal and was prepared to work hard and liked working in the kitchen. I rather nervously explained to Mrs Anderson that this was the only person I could find. All she said was: 'Don't worry. I will have a saucepan ready to bang him on the head if need be!'

We used to give Henry his baths in a big old tub in front of the fire. From the very first moment he had his own personality and was the dominant person in the house. Henry looked exactly like his father and was quite fair, while all my family are dark with ink black hair. He was very attractive as a little boy but always wanted to grow up too fast.

It wasn't long before I was pregnant again and his nose was rather put out of joint when Louisa Jane was born on 8th January 1955, as she was a very handsome child. Louisa looked like me with dark hair and an alabaster complexion. She was shy and quite difficult while Henry was easy and full of life. He was very independent and would go off into the garden by himself for hours, or turn up in the kitchen demanding a steak. He chummed up with the driver and his wife and you could usually find him there eating sweets.

When Richard Winston Mark was born on 3rd July 1956 he weighed over nine pounds and arrived in a very short time. He also looked like my family with enormous black eyes and long eyelashes. He was quite irresistible as a child and I tried not to favouritise him. Our family was now complete. We loved our babies, and the farm was paying like mad as the post-war agriculture boom got into its stride. I waited until Richard was born and then had all the children christened together in the little local church. Henry's godparents were Gena Phillips, Elizabeth Northumberland, Andrew Scott, Peter Chance and

Francis Egerton. For his first birthday Mrs Anderson made a wonderful birthday cake decorated with a huge skating scene. I am so sorry I never took a photograph of it.

Erland was a good father, very calm, quiet and loving. I think he became obsessed with the children and, instead of entertaining all the world in those years, we were very happy at home. In any case it was hard to get people to come and stay as there weren't very good transport links to Cambridge in those days. The children didn't go to nursery school and ate in the nursery with Nanny. I hired a French nursery maid who I thought was rather jolly, but the children and other staff disliked her as she hardly spoke any English. One day Henry got hold of her bottle of scent and flung it out of the window and she didn't last long after that. The nursery remained a cosy domain for everyone to go to when worried or needing a plaster.

We had such fun with the children making little houses out of the stooks of corn at harvest time and playing golf. We had inherited this enormous swimming pool from when the house had been a school, and it was a priority to teach the children to swim so they would be safe playing in the garden. Otherwise it would have been a permanent anxiety. I got a pony and taught them to ride, which they adored, although sadly there was no hunting around Cambridge, unlike in the shires.

Our life became more and more embracing and exciting as we got to know our neighbours. There were lots of interesting people in the vicinity including Victor Rothschild and his wife Tess, whom I found fascinating. They were totally brilliant and full of the arts. I met them at a dinner party at Duff and Diana Cooper's. Our immediate neighbours were the Adeanes. Robert Adeane was the friend who had persuaded Erland to buy West Wratting in the first place. The Sutherland family, whom I hardly knew at first, then owned an enormous acreage round Newmarket. They were always there, along with the Vesteys, who had vast lands all over the world and were a great beef producing family. Lastly there was Sir Arthur Marshall, who had created Marshall's airfield at Cambridge, where decades later the nose of Concorde was changed.

Erland's brother used to come to stay but because he didn't shoot they didn't have so much in common. His son, Erland's nephew Mike d'Abo, was a very original and musical little boy, who achieved fame as the lead vocalist of the pop group Manfred Mann. The night before his mother's funeral he composed a beautiful piece of music to be played at the little local church. He continues to perform with the Manfreds and it is always a pleasure to hear him sing at family gatherings. His daughter Olivia is an actress who made her name in *The Wonder Years*. In 2008 at the age of sixty-three Mike became the father of twins Ella and Louis with his third wife Lisa.

Mike's cousin Maryam from the French side of the family was an exquisitely pretty girl who came to visit when I was living in my lovely Georgian house in Kensington Square which I will explain later. She sat in the kitchen sweetly curled up in a chair and talked about her hopes and dreams. In 1987 she was cast by the director John Glen as a Russian cellist in the James Bond movie, *The Living Daylights*, and her life changed forever. She eventually married Hugh Hudson, the director of *Chariots of Fire*.

I found Mr Mayhew, a marvellous gardener of the old school who had been trained as a garden boy in a big estate. He could grow more or less anything but had no help, not even a garden boy, so I became the factotum. I was still physically weak but rose above it as I loved my gardens. He was brilliant at grafting and we produced and sold vegetables to the town and we actually made a profit, especially with our tomatoes. After this commercial success Mr Mayhew perhaps concentrated a little less on my flower garden and potplants.

I saw none of my friends because I was working so hard. Bathrooms were fitted from scratch. The parapets on the roof were fitted with a lead gutter which leaked after snow storms when the lead would fracture. I found the old established firm of Rattee & Kett in Cambridge to sort out many of these problems. They had looked after King's College Chapel for ever.

My sister Isabel left Loel Guinness in 1951 and started her own art gallery in Arthingworth with her divorce settlement. She was entrepreneurial and rather successful in buying and selling middle range British paintings. She and Loel were not really compatible as he wanted to go yachting all the time with fashionable people like the Windsors and spend the weekends in their house in Normandy. She was happy with her two children Billy, William Loel Seymour, born 28th December 1939, and Lindy, Serena Belinda Rosemary, born 25th March 1941. Isabel ended up marrying her old friend Sir Robert Throckmorton, Bart. as her second husband in 1953. She then ran her gallery from Coughton Court, in Warwickshire, the Throckmorton home run by the National Trust.

One day I had a surprise visit from Lord Brownlow and the man who gave me my first kiss. It was a burning hot summer's day and they were both elderly, overweight men. I laughed to see them sitting in the children's paddling pool, and they couldn't believe I was happily married with three wonderful children and the house was so beautiful.

Henry was always out on a limb of his own. Louisa and Richard were closer in age and had their own trials and tribulations. The only day I left them with an Australian girl to go up to London I returned home to be greeted by Louisa on the front door holding one of Richard's little shoes full of blood. They had had a row on the tennis court and he had stormed off, kicked the Orangery door open and cut his leg. He was whisked off to Addenbrooke's Hospital where a rather forbidding matron said: 'What have you been doing, you silly little boy! Come here and I'll stitch you up'.

By then Erland was making a great success of his work in the City so we had enough money. He would come home religiously most evenings and when he it wasn't possible would stay in my little flat in London. He went abroad a lot and made money in various parts of Africa. He was forever finding new things to do in the business world. My brother Charles was very interested in what he was doing and they flew out to see a mine in Africa in which he hoped to invest. I was furious because they left me alone, heavily pregnant with my first baby. They flew in a new, not completely proven airliner, so I was even more worried.

Spain was another area where he was interested, but that was not a success. He thought he could make vast sums of money out of some land north of Marbella in southern Spain. He had made friends with the Palade family who owned the land but they turned out to be completely phoney. I kept saying to Erland: 'You know that Mrs Palade only waters her plants once a month and pulls the loo very rarely'. Somehow he convinced Erland there was water on the land, and we even went out and had a celebration with the three children wearing sombreros as we watched the water flowing. It turned out that the water was diverted from the next village! He had three sons and dressed like an English gentleman and had two beautiful houses in the mountains. Erland completely believed in it and didn't listen to me. To beguile me Palade used to bring me vast bunches of flowers in the colour of the Spanish flag whenever he came to London.

I loathed the place because I thought it was dangerous for the children. The road was on a precipice and only two cars could pass. Only the very rich had houses there then. Eventually they brought water in a huge pipe from the mains at Cadiz to the whole coast and the whole coastline exploded. By that time we were bust and sold up there. The distance from one village to another in those mountains was vast. Now it's cheek by jowl and you can't buy a square foot.

The English side of it was the Marbella Club. I never wanted the children to go there. I saw them moving a sewage pipe so it would go into the bay where they were all swimming, regardless. There was a famous bullfighting ring at Ronda made entirely of huge old stones, with a gap all the way around the ring. I don't really know what the business transactions were between my husband and the Palade family. All I know is we lost our shirts because of the lack of water. By that time all the children were at prep schools and I was living at West Wratting and going to London now and then.

I had a flat in London called Park West, off the Edgware Road, before I married, and I kept it on as a pied-à-terre and for Erland to use when the weather was too bad for him to come home to West Wratting. After so many years and the boys going to prep schools I decided we ought to have something bigger in London. I saw a sign up in Kensington Square behind Derry & Toms and decided to investigate. I walked round the square and found a lovely big family house on the corner for sale. It would have been a wonderful investment but I couldn't manage it, so I rented the first house I saw at No. 29 for five years. It had a terribly pretty door with a lift from the basement to the top floor, period panelling and big fireplaces. It also had the word 'Condemned' attached to it, but I was absolutely determined to have it. A small bomb had taken part of the top floor so I had to undertake a lot more construction to make it safe. It was very hard work for me but it became a dream family house.

When the lease came to an end I was paying a tiny rent. I bravely walked in on the Crown Estate Office which seemed to stretch from Trafalgar Square to the Houses of Parliament. The man who was in charge of the whole Kensington area had an office which seemed two miles long. You could have skated on the boardroom table. He was two thumbs high with grey whiskers coming down from his cheeks and his ears. He then proceeded to roll out all the maps of the area on this huge table, much to my amazement. I wish I could have bought all these island estates, I would have made a fortune as they were all falling down. I said: 'Why can't I have this house as it was derelict?' I bought it for £25,000 and he helped me in every way he could. The house suited Erland as he would walk through Derry and Toms every morning and all the ladies would smile at him. He would then get on the tube at Kensington High Street straight to Liverpool Street, which was a stone's throw from his office in Throgmorton Street.

We entertained a good deal with small dinners as I hate cocktail parties. It was quite a safe area with the communal garden for the children and the people in the square became a nice community of friends. My mother wrote to me: 'Why do you have to have two houses in the country?' – because in her day Kensington was the country.

144

Chapter Ten
The Husband Collector

In the midst of this domestic idyll I gradually became aware of the fact that this husband of mine had been collected by a woman about eight feet high, beautifully proportioned and very intelligent, but with huge spatula feet. I shall call her The Mistress. She was an only child, without a penny in the world but she had a millionaire lover. She was considered very elegant and sexy, but the only thing in her heart was a passion for money, success, achievement and social advancement at any cost. She settled on Erland, and when the millionaire found out what she was up to he more or less discarded her, or treated her as one of many, as those men do.

She was a home-breaker. She was about to leave a very rich man and she wanted marriage again. Unfortunately they met at a time when Erland was going through the change of life and ill-health, so I think he was very vulnerable. She made Erland write a letter to me saying he wanted a divorce.

When I found out about this I was absolutely horrified and terribly sad, because we had been so happy for many years. I suppose I had let myself go living in the country and working on the farm. I had been concentrating on West Wratting and had to have so many plastic surgery operations on my face while giving birth to three children in as many years. He always wanted me to go away for weekends, socialising with people like the Queen of Holland, but I had created a wonderful home for him and wanted to stay there, as I was passionately in love with the children, the farm and the garden. I felt I was a total wreck and never had the right clothes for these escapades.

One of our neighbours, Lady Delamere, used always to flirt with Erland. She was very unattractive with red hair and quite old. When she came to lunch she would always say to Erland: 'I'm all the better for seeing you'. Our parrot picked it up and would repeat it endlessly and the children were in guffaws of laughter. When the doorbell rang I used to chase them down the corridor, giggling and clutching the parrot so she wouldn't hear. Lady Delamere was in ecstasy when she heard about The Mistress. She said: 'You must use our famous and wonderful family solicitor who also acts for Louis Mountbatten'. But I

146

didn't want a solicitor and I didn't want a divorce, I just wanted my husband back.

I decided to ask advice from a famous judge called Howard who lived in the vicinity. I begged him to intervene and speak to Erland. He said: 'Do you know, Lady Ursula, I have heard so many cases of a similar nature but never thought Erland would succumb as you always seemed so happy together. I wouldn't have believed it of Erland, but men obviously get this thing at a certain age and then proceed to tell their wives every detail about it'. That was absolutely true as Erland had subjected me to endless stories about his fascination for this woman. Judge Howard recommended a line of least resistance and said: 'Just let it run its course. If you stay quiet he may grow out of it'. So Erland moved in with her in London and I was left alone with the children in the country.

One night the telephone rang and who do you think was on it? The Mistress' lover, Paul Getty, who was said to be the richest man in the world. He asked me if we were really estranged, my husband and I. I said 'No, but for this wretched woman who is a well known home breaker!' and put the telephone down. I tried not to encourage him but used to call in desperation to find out what was his situation with this woman. From that moment on Paul pursued me.

One evening she asked Erland and me for drinks and dinner in London. Can you imagine how ghastly it was pretending to be civilised but dying inside? Off we went to dinner and the food was very good as she was an excellent cook, but she had a heart made of metal, all based on money. I had fallen down so I couldn't get upstairs to powder my nose with all the ladies, when they left the gentlemen to drink their port. So I sat in the little library gloomily meditating on my ailments. When I looked up I saw the bureau bookcase and something clicked. I suddenly remembered Erland telling me he had written to her at every minute of the day, and she used to keep his letters tied up in a blue ribbon in a secret drawer of her desk. I thought: 'My goodness, if my ankle permits I shall get up and open it'. I would know how to find it because all the bureaux at home had secret, funny little drawers which we used to play with as children. I quickly found the bundle with the blue ribbon, took it out and slipped it into my purse and said nothing.

Eventually Erland and I went home and I will never forget wanting to say something in the car, but I had had a lot to drink and was very tired and upset. I woke up in the morning but he had already gone to work and I suddenly thought of the letters. I read them from cover to cover and was absolutely horrified. With tears running down my face I burned them to a crisp in a saucepan.

Sir David Hill-Ward arranged for us to go for a week's holiday with the children to Spain. Off we all bundled and Erland was very charming indeed, couldn't have been sweeter. The children had a lovely time until one day we got stuck in a lift. Erland was lying in the sun reading but the children and I wanted to go to the beach so headed to the lift which was carved into the rock face. Half way down it got stuck with just the children and me and a French man. Nothing would move this lift and it was boiling hot. I have never been so frightened. We really thought we were going to die there unless somebody came to help. What seemed like hours later, but in reality was probably about forty minutes, a man finally appeared. What do you think he said: 'We were just working on the lift and didn't bother to put up a sign. So sorry'. My heart was palpitating and I was in a terrible state and hated the whole holiday from that moment on.

Erland drove us home and appeared to be perfectly all right. For the last five years he had had a heart problem which was hereditary in the family. His father had died of it. However there was no doubt that Erland would continue shooting and doing all the things he loved.

On our return we had been invited to a friend's wedding. In the church Erland insisted on kneeling throughout the service. We had a very late supper and I drove home. On the way he complained about not feeling well and I was dead beat after a day of duty so we went straight to bed. That night, 30th July 1970, I was lying beside him in the bed when I suddenly heard a roar like thunder. I never knew having a heart attack was so incredibly loud. I was startled awake to find my dear husband dead beside me. The shock combination of him leaving me, coming back and now this was almost more than I could bear. Louisa came rushing down the stairs because she adored him and nearly passed out, which made it even worse. I had already experienced sudden death with my darling father at Belvoir and now this. It was too much. He was only fifty-eight years old.

Henry, aged sixteen, was old enough to cope well as I passed out with horror, and dear Louisa was in the same state as me. Henry behaved like a fully grown man and took over all the organisation together. We buried my beloved husband at West Wratting and my friend Mr Hyslop, of the Cambridge stonemasons Rattee & Kett, designed a triangular headstone of great beauty. Paul Hyslop was well known because he worked on the baldacchino above the altar by Stephen Dykes Bower of 1949-58 at St Paul's Cathedral, inspired by Sir Christopher Wren. I used to take Henry to see this, and Paul Hyslop later helped me design the library at West Wratting.

Eventually Paul Getty left The Mistress, but with some money because he said she would be on the dole otherwise. When Erland died Paul made a beeline for me and my life switched just like that. I was feeling miserable because of the breaking up of my home and house so I just let it drift. I stayed at West Wratting walking in the gardens, playing with my Doberman dog, Mr Blue, and just trying to forget. In the end I felt so lost and lonely I fell for this dear old man's kindness and charm, which were legion. He treated me like the Queen and took me everywhere. He wanted to visit all the loveliest houses in England, which we did, and he took me to amusing things in London as well as dreadful things like boxing arenas, which he adored. He didn't hurry me until one day he said: 'You had better come away with me to Italy.'

Chapter Eleven
Escapades

The children were away at boarding school and I took a deep breath and decided to pack up shop and run away with Paul to Italy. He said it would be lovely if we went by car but he didn't drive so I volunteered the beautiful Mercedes which Erland had given me not long ago. I thought we would leave happily from London, but not at all. He insisted on going to Paris to visit Paul-Louis Valère, or some such grandee who was giving a ball in Paris to which he had been bidden. I didn't even know the man and nobody knew that I knew Paul. Then I found out that he was going to this ball with the Duchess of Argyll. It broke my heart and I nearly abandoned the whole trip. Somehow I found myself collecting him like a chauffeur after the party in Paris and off we went zooming down all the way to Cannes with me behind the wheel. I am a fast driver!

We hadn't realised that because of the Film Festival it would be difficult to find accommodation. We couldn't get a room anywhere so headed across the border to an extraordinary Italian villa. I was had up for speeding on the way because Paul always wanted me to go quicker and quicker out of terror of being shot or kidnapped. It was only then that I realised I was being used as a woman decoy in a lovely Mercedes. I told Paul not to speak but just sit quietly and let me deal with it.

Life with Paul was a world of complete theatre, as exciting as a thriller, and I just had to know the latest development. Norris phoned ahead for us to be met at another of Paul's villas. We drove for miles and miles and eventually came to the villa where I was to stay for about three weeks. As we came into the main entrance there standing in the drive was a woman of about forty years old. Her name was Rosabella Burch, a curvy Nicaraguan widow, who was Paul's third, fourth or fifth mistress. Apparently all his other girlfriends from the past were going to converge on me for a holiday. It was the most ghastly situation I had even been in and I simply couldn't stand it. I told Paul I would pack up and go home. He had told me about his women, whom he claimed were all for a specific purpose. I think Rosabella was his manicurist. The only one that really counted was The Mistress, who was really attractive but didn't have any morals. Her parents had been killed in the war and she didn't have a penny.

I was shown up to a room in the villa, which was nowhere near Paul's, as clearly planned by Rosabella. I shed a tear and thought: 'What on earth shall I do now? Perhaps I'd better just give the whole thing up and drive away right now'. But I was exhausted from the long drive and didn't know quite where to go. Had I known I wouldn't have even stayed one hour. The next day Paul realised how I felt and was unbelievably nice to me. He said: 'You are really special to me. None of the others matter, they are just my mistresses. I look at it like owning a toothbrush'. I did eventually meet all of them and Rosabella was the one I liked best as she was a very warm person. His nickname for me was Little Bear, because Ursa is the Latin word for bear. Once when I tore the sleeve of my blouse he said to me: 'Poor Little Bear is threadbare'. He really was the most charming, ordinary man, made into this monster by journalists.

I eventually believed Paul and stayed on and we had the most marvellous time although the villa was too awful: a pompous, ghastly building of great age but no charm, perched on a rock above a beach with no sand. There was no good bay nearby but there was a beautiful long terrace with a balustrade where you could walk and sense the wonder of the ocean. I had imagined a lovely sandy beach and cosy little Italian village with rustic restaurants, but Paul felt the location was more secure.

Paul told me he had been summoned for the weekend on a business trip to Naples with Rosabella and Norris, instead of which he decided to go with me. 'I am not taking Mr Bramlett and that's why I want you to drive me', he claimed. I died of horror at the thought of another long journey. Bizarrely his plan was that I would drive while a British chauffeur came with us as a passenger in the back seat for security. Rosabella screamed and yelled at the thought of not going to Naples but to no avail. After all, I was seated beside Paul every night for dinner with someone of his allocation on my other side. He was such a charming, honest and old fashioned fellow, almost too good to be true. We entertained various businessmen who seemed to me to be crooks, but I suppose they flattered Paul in some way.

We set off for Naples and found our way to the house where he expected to have this business meeting. He told me to stay in the car and went to investigate with the detective, but nobody was there except the housekeeper. When they looked in the fridge and saw how much food was stuffed in there, Paul came out white as a sheet saying it had been a setup and they were planning to hold him as a hostage. We sped off to the Palazzo Caracciolo Hotel in Naples where I had stayed with my father, but it was impossible to get a room so it was back to the villa.

I took lovely long walks every day until one afternoon I came home to a dreadful commotion with Paul accusing Rosabella of having an affair with Norris, who was defending her. It was all terribly convoluted and I couldn't stand it any more. On 28th June the children were coming out from school for their summer holidays and I told Paul I had got to be there. I said I would fly back to London, although he was very reluctant and miserable.

We threw our things into suitcases and headed off in one car with Norris and a detective and the rest of the luggage in a car ahead of us. Meanwhile poor Rosabella was so incensed that when we got to the outer gate we saw her riding furiously on a bicycle behind us like the Wicked Witch of the West. She was going so fast I was worried she would drive into the back of us. Paul just said cavalierly: 'Drive on!' and we left her shouting and pedalling madly in the receding distance. I had no idea where we were going. I thought we were going back to London but Paul had other plans.

He had me drive in one day all the way to Lake Lugano to the Villa Favorita, where he had decided we were going to stay with Heini Thyssen. Paul refused to drive. Frankly it was just as well since not only was he seventy-five years old but was terrified of everything. We had a slight accident because I was very tired and quite distraught, and I think must have closed my eyes for a minute. I was following the other car, which Norris was driving, through a crossroads and got a terrible shock when I hit a small car slightly. I managed to turn the Mercedes off the road and slide around on the grass. Luckily the other driver was fine and my car wasn't destroyed but I couldn't get it to start. Nothing would move it. This was very unlike me but I was exhausted as he made me motor non stop from Naples, without even stopping for a meal, because he was worried about being followed and shot.

Norris and the detective saw what happened and they whisked Paul off in their car, while I was left with the valet, trembling with shock and fatigue in the middle of a muddy field. He sat having a drink in the hotel in Lugano with the wretched Norris while I had to organise getting Mercedes to pick up the car. Luckily I knew the people at Mercedes in Europe because the car had originally come from Germany. It was an extraordinary episode but I think after the war nothing could shock me. I did manage to sort everything and eventually went to the hotel where Paul was waiting for me with great concern. 'For God's sake get me a drink', I exclaimed. A placatory large dry martini duly arrived. Paul then rang Heini Thyssen to tell him what had happened and he told us to come immediately to his villa.

From the Villa Favorita Heini sent me back to London in his own plane and I had a rapturous reunion with the children. I decided not to contact Paul but the next day he turned up at the front door without ringing and said simply: 'You must come to the theatre with me' and we were back as we were before. He couldn't bear to be alone, night or day. Let's face it, he had received the ear of his grandson in a paper bag. He came back to West Wratting with us and saw the house in its glory at harvest time. The children loved building little houses out of the bales of straw and I would make picnics to have in the fields. Scones, sandwiches, bananas and ginger cake with sugar icing would all be carefully packed in baskets and shared with friends and neighbours. Nowadays the process is so mechanical you don't even see a crumb left on a harvested field.

I taught the children to drive at the bottom of one of the fields, in my Mini in a course I constructed with red barrels. Dick was so tiny you couldn't see his face above the steering wheel and it looked as though the car was being driven by a robot. The children got to know Paul. Soon everybody knew, as the press followed every move he made. Norris was in on all of it to his dying day and would pick up on anything to destroy me.

Paul told me all about his mother who was the most dominant person in his life. She was brilliant in every way and very loving. His father was a lawyer but went into the oil business. They would travel to New York together to do deals at the beginning of that expanding industry when it was unregulated. He said it felt like being a cowboy in the frontiers of the Wild West, with beautiful girls appearing at your side mesmerised by the smell of new money.

When the children went back to school I went to live with Paul. When Erland had been alive Paul had visited us at West Wratting with his son and sat on the terrace one day looking out on the wonderful view with cows grazing and not a sight of anything modern. He said to me: 'One day I will have my own place like this.' I wasn't in a position to deal with him at that time as I was happily married. Now he was settled at Sutton Place near Guildford, a perfect house built in about 1530 for a courtier of Henry VIII. It used to belong to Geordie, Duke of Sutherland, whom I knew well and used to visit there. Everybody knew Paul because he had been a Rhodes scholar at Oxford and was an Anglophile. He didn't want to go back to America because he was terrified of flying and of being murdered. So he bought Sutton Place. We lived there as though married for five years until he died. I used to go for the day either to West Wratting or to my house in Kensington Square, but

Paul made me promise to get back to Sutton Place at night.

The children got on well with Paul, especially Richard, my youngest, who was at Eton at the time. We often went to watch him play cricket, football and the Wall Game and Paul really enjoyed all the Eton festivities. The Headmaster's wife would join us for picnics and when the sun shone there was nothing more gloriously English. Paul was fond of Richard, who was sporty and popular and eventually elected a member of Pop. He promised to help Richard get a job when he left school but sadly was not to live long enough. He wanted to give a ball for Louisa when she turned seventeen, a grand coming-out dance at Sutton Place. I am ashamed to say I turned him down flat and never breathed a word to Louisa because I didn't think it would help her socially. I loved Paul but at the same time I felt rather embarrassed about our relationship, I suppose because of his reputation and all the other women involved in his life. At the same time he could be very cosy and charming, and loved coming to have a simple supper in the nursery at 29 Kensington Square.

Before he ever met me Paul had read a book called *Dorothy Vernon of Haddon Hall*, a romantic historical novel written in 1902 by Charles Major. It tells the story of how in the year 1550 eighteen year old Dorothy, the daughter of Sir George Vernon of

Haddon Hall, fell in love with John Manners, the second son of the 1st Earl of Rutland, against their families' wishes. They endured many adventures in their quest to be together. The story even included the young Elizabeth I and Mary Queen of Scots. In 1924 it was turned into a silent movie starring Mary Pickford and Anders Randolf and directed by Marshall Neilan. Now Paul produced this book, about which I knew nothing. He was fascinated to visit the place where it was set and I arranged to take him to Haddon Hall to meet Mother there.

Louisa and I drove up to Derbyshire with Paul in his car one Saturday morning, slowly wending our way through the heather, over Beeley Moor, just east of Haddon. I started talking about the bees I had tended during the war and how I had brought them to that heather so the honey would be scented. When we arrived Mother was already there to greet us and despite my trepidation they got on like a house on fire. Paul was determined to see every aspect of the house and we took him into all the rooms and even up onto the roof, which was rather dangerous at his age because of the slippery tiles, and the beautiful gardens. Mother and I talked to him at length about the restoration and how she lay on buttresses planting diminutive creeping plants on the walls. He was obsessed with the fact that John Manners, who wasn't considered suitable in any way, did marry

Dorothy Vernon in the end, and that's how the property came into our family.

On Sunday his rather large and vulgar American car and chauffeur took us to Chatsworth, the Dukes of Devonshire's house, which was just over our garden wall, to collect Louisa who had been staying there. As she emerged from the kitchen through an awning of roses she was attacked by a swarm of bees. The chauffeur, Lee, tried to brush them off but was stung himself. Moucher Devonshire, widow of the 10th Duke, ran out in horror and pandemonium reigned. Suddenly Moucher's dachshund appeared and started frantically rushing around, and it turned out she had been stung on every nipple. We all got the giggles, although it was not funny for poor Louisa, whom we had to drive to the hospital to have an injection for the shock and swelling. We all ended up at Haddon for tea in a state of exhaustion. The weekend over, we motored back to London and Mother returned to Belvoir, where she was living at that time.

Although Sutton Place was a beautiful house I always thought the atmosphere rather creepy. The Mistress had bought the house for him, engaged all the servants and ran the place for him, along with the very impressive female secretary and his doctor. The butler, Bullimore, was nominally in charge, and ran the roost with his male friend. They were in touch with The Mistress and the other women, but the doctor gradually became more and more important in the power play at Sutton. The cook was charming in an old fashioned way but was constrained in his budgeting by Paul, who never wanted the house to cost more than a certain figure every year. As a result the food was satisfactory, hardly meagre, but there were no barons of beef on the sideboard. As Paul grew older and weaker I suggested putting a lift into the house and found the best spot in the cellar. I was told categorically it was impossible because that was where Bullimore sat for his breaks, immediately under the study. This was where Paul would be closeted for hours with Norris, who had been appointed by his American company to look after him.

All his various children and grandchildren came to stay at times and we would go for long walks after lunch. I longed to invite my friends but there was usually a very business-like atmosphere at lunch and dinner, to which were summoned a constant stream of leading industrialists and financial associates. Very few people saw the kind, cosy side of Paul as more often than not he was on guard when he mixed in society. He was clever and used to study Latin grammar at breakfast. He never need a note at a meeting but had all the figures in his head. You could see that independent mind working away constantly. At the same time he was very demanding and easily bored. You couldn't just say you played the piano unless you did so superlatively. Music was one of his passions and he was a great friend of Leonard Bernstein, to whom I was thrilled to be introduced at one of his concerts.

He took great pleasure in adopting the sartorial habits of an English country gentleman without actually doing any shooting, hunting or fishing. He was bewitched by the beauty of the great English stately homes. He loved the sea and had had a passion for surfing as a young man. He would occasionally drink champagne but his libation of choice was Rum and Coke, which he always had at his side, even on his bedside table. I never mentioned money to Paul. He would sometimes give me a case of champagne or a nice Christmas present but he lived as frugally as a Scotsman. He used to say: 'You are not rich until you cannot count your money any more'. Where his wealth gave him enjoyment was the ability to invest in business ventures – that is what he felt was the point of it. He proposed to me and told me he would leave me a vast inheritance.

I actually felt quite sorry for Paul. He was constantly terrified of being blown up or shot. The wealth he had inherited from his mother had not brought him happiness and was tainted with the horror of his grandson's ear being cut off. It is a horrid feeling to think that you are always being watched and followed. He never wanted to go in an airplane or a boat. I never went to ski resorts with him. In cars he would shout 'Go faster, faster...' and never said why. I realised that really big money is not a joy, certainly not in this era. I believe if you have great wealth you can bribe almost anybody and you can never trust the people around you.

All the time Paul was being given pills and phials that arrived from America and were dispensed by the doctor. The doctor had been telling Paul that I was bad for him and that he should break with me. One day they all got together and surrounded me, saying: 'You've got to go because you are endangering Paul's health'. Although I suspected this confrontation was coming because Paul had warned me, I was shocked they accused me of that. It was a short while after lunch. After that memorable interview they went away and I went to my room, desperate to see Paul. One of the staff came into my room and said: 'Lady Ursula, you must go'. Furiously, I threw some things in a suitcase and went downstairs where the detective and everybody was waiting to see me off. I was determined not to go without a showdown. I tried to object but the youngest detective said: 'You're trespassing and you have to go now'. He always had a gun on him and I was terrified.

I was never allowed back. As Paul got sicker and sicker I was determined to see him because I loved him. His bed was on the ground floor and he was being looked after by a nurse who was married to one of his entourage. They tried to stop me getting in and the dogs came sniffing around but they loved me. I went up to the window where he was lying in his office and banged on the window. He tried to get up when he saw me and eventually they let me in through the door. All his favourite books had been taken out of his bedroom which now looked like an operating theatre. The Mistress was already married to someone else but came back when she heard Paul was dying.

I came back the next day and they were all whispering in his ears. He dropped back in the bed, as if acknowledging everything I had said was right, but I knew he would have left me in the end. So I went in despair, knowing I would never see him again. He died three months later in June 1976. I still miss him. He was a total lady-killer but physically very strong despite his age, and he made you feel like the only person in the world when you were with him. He had a great sense of fun.

I was the one who told him he must go into North Sea oil and he said: 'You're the most expensive girlfriend I have ever had.' I suppose he thought I wanted the outcome of the North Sea oil but I loved him for himself and never wanted any of his money. We never talked about money except in terms of the new business developments in the world and exciting experiments. It was a great shock when Paul died, even though I knew it was coming and they had precipitated it with all kind of drugs. He was eighty-three years old and it was reported as heart failure. I was asked to go to the funeral but I was so distressed I couldn't bear it.

I went back to West Wratting; to Nelson and Emily, my Portuguese couple, and my darling Doberman, Mr Blue. I fell in love with him when I saw him in the street walking with a friend of mind. She saw how we instantly bonded and said: 'Will you take him? I'm getting married soon and I can't cope with him'. So he walked into the lift of my house in Kensington Square and made himself instantly at home. He wouldn't let anyone near me that he didn't like and was such a solace to have around when I was alone.

Chapter Twelve
Derby Dreams

1989 was a period in my life when I felt very sad and lonely. I spent most of my time gloomily walking in the country, trying to get over the shock of everything that had happened in my life, talking to my lovely Doberman. One day Richard rang me and said he had met a famous racehorse trainer called John Gosden, who was English but for the last few years had been based in Los Angeles. He was about to return to Newmarket to train horses for one of the wealthy Arab families that dominated the sport. Richard had decided he would give me a horse to cheer me up. I was delighted although I wondered how he would be able to afford it. In the end my son's persistence won me over and I thought the least I could do was to meet him.

I went to lunch with Gosden and his wife Rachel, who was a trained lawyer. He was very tall and handsome, dressed in racing tweeds and very sure of himself. He said he had a horse I could buy and showed me the pedigree. I had been a good judge of horses all my life, having practically grown up in the saddle, and when I realised it had the illustrious Hyperion in its bloodline I started to get very excited. There was a life-size bronze statue of Hyperion by John Skeaping belonging to Lord Derby which stood in front of the Jockey Club in Newmarket. You were not welcome unless you were a member, but since West Wratting was practically next door I viewed them as simply my neighbours.

Richard knew I had always longed to have a racehorse from the days when my husband and I started to live at West Wratting. My family were used to having horses and had owned since 1750 a beautiful 17th century house, Cheveley Park, near Newmarket. In 1828 the 5th Duke of Rutland had won the Derby with Cadland, and it was in my blood. Unfortunately the Belvoir agent of the day was crooked and sold more or less the whole acreage of the Cheveley estate, lot by lot. In the end the family got rid of it, it caught fire and was demolished around 1900. Erland and I sat down and made the decision we could never afford racehorses and that was that.

I couldn't believe I would now own my own racehorse. Richard bought the horse for me, but refused to tell me what he paid. When I went to visit it for the first time I ran my hand down its fetlock and I am sure the trainer thought I was mad. This beautiful animal, believe it or not, looked at me and crossed its two front feet and I was totally charmed. It had a reputation for being unmanageable and the trainer didn't want me anywhere near it. It was incredibly talented but never wanted to do anything it was told. I felt a secret empathy with its proud, fighting spirit. It was handsome, small and stocky like Hyperion, and didn't have the appearance of a great horse but possessed wonderful spring and was strong. It was a chestnut with a white diamond on its forehead and two white fetlocks. I wished I could have gone to see it being taken out on the gallop but I was too busy and preoccupied. I had to find a name for it. Richard always called Paul PG Tips, because he looked like the caricature, and that is what we christened the horse.

It was extremely interesting to follow PG Tips' training and finally Gosden entered it for its first race, which was at Wolverhampton on a dirt surface. I had been to Ascot dressed up to the nines but this wasn't at all how I visualised racing; it was all new to me. Wolverhampton was one of those extraordinary modern racetracks where you can have supper and see whichever race you want to on a small television in front of you. It was rather like a huge football stadium with various stands and all the amenities you could wish, not exactly smart but very down to earth, the opposite of grand. It was more like drinking a glass of beer in the local pub than quaffing champagne in the Owners' Enclosure. There were bookies everywhere and nobody was well dressed.

I was taken by Rachel Gosden, her mother-in-law and the Queen's trainer, Lord Porchester. Gosden's mother kept saying, 'You know, Lady Ursula, you are not really dressed for a winner'. I was aware I had let myself go looking after children, houses and dogs. But Porchester laughed and said I was perfectly attired for Wolverhampton. It didn't win that first time but every other time it ran it did, bar the very last race. I didn't gamble on the outcome, not once.

The first time I had gambled was in the 1930s when I met Nico 'Nicky' Zographos, the head of the Greek Syndicate and owner of the casino at Cannes who ran Tout Va - banque ouverte. There was no sum of money he wouldn't stake at the baccarat table. I was staying with a great friend of my father, Madame Edvina, a prominent Montreal-born opera star who sang with Caruso and had great success at Covent Garden. She had retired to Cannes and owned an antique store on the Croisette. She was highly educated and I think my father thought I would have a cultural holiday. I was only seventeen but everything was done through friendship in that small well-knit society. Instead I befriended a lot of immensely rich Russians who had escaped from the revolution, and was taken up by Sybil, the Marchioness of Cholmondeley, jewels to the elbow. Zographus pushed over a mammoth amount of chips and I never stopped winning.

I went back to England aglow with my success and immediately bought a new hunter. Soon my winnings had disappeared and I pleaded with my father: 'Darling Daddy, can I go to Cannes again?' Inevitably I lost and went back to my father in tears but there was no help forthcoming. He said wryly: 'I am not going to pay your debts and that will cure you of gambling, once and for all'. And it did. In the end the Duke of Gloucester, who often rode in the Belvoir Hunt, realised my dilemma and came to my aid by buying the hunter from me. As things progressed it became obvious how expensive the whole racing venture was. I had no money and Richard was up and down in his business enterprise. The purchase price of the horse was nothing compared to the costs of vets, trainers, looseboxes, Jockey Club membership, choosing the colours of the silks and registering its name. Very sadly we had to say goodbye to PG Tips after three years. We were lucky that with the small sums it won during its career the whole venture broke even. Not many owners can claim that.

If I ever have a racehorse again I shall keep it at home like Signorinetta. Signorinetta, who won the Derby in 1908, was owned and trained by Cavaliere Edoardo Ginistrelli. The famous royal trainer Sir Cecil Boyd-Rochfort came to lunch at West Wratting and told me the whole story of how Ginistrelli would play the barrel organ to Signorinetta and go alongside the rails and talk to her at the beginning of each race. In all my years of hunting I had learned that horses would do as you wished if you talked to them and established a personal rapport. I was very lucky to ride a brilliant hunter. 'Come on darling Dobbin. We're for it now!' I would cry out as we sailed over the hedges. I knew he would do whatever I wished.

Nowadays I watch the Derby on television and when the horses are being paraded without their saddles I try to predict the winner. In 2011 I was alone in my flat feeling quite gloomy about life in general. I wasn't paying much attention until I looked back with a jerk and saw a most wonderful horse. As they were in the parade ring I saw the number 9, which was my lucky number, and realised it was a beautiful French horse called Pour Moi trained by André Fabre, who had a reputation for being excellent but difficult. The jockey was the talented nineteen year old Mickael Barzalona. The combination of all this, and the fact that Pour Moi means For Me made me decide to have a bet. It had enormous odds of ten to one and I was going to put £50,000 on it and risk everything. I desperately rang friends who had accounts at Ladbrokes but couldn't get in touch with anyone in time. In the final stretch Barzalona was holding the bridle tight, standing up in his stirrups and waving over the winning line, and they said he would be disqualified, but he won by a head at four to one, against the favourite, the Queen's horse Treasure Beach. A truly memorable Derby.

Chapter Thirteen
The Next Generation

The children were growing up fast which fascinated me. Richard was tall, energetic and handsome and was in Pop at Eton. Henry had left Eton and was working at Messel's. Henry travelled a lot and had a wonderful time, bringing lots of friends to stay at West Wratting. Louisa was at a very good Catholic school and enjoying it enormously. She wanted to be a tennis player and a little bit of everything and was pretty. My London house in Kensington Square became a centre for the young. My Portuguese couple were in the London house when I wasn't there. The young people had a whale of a time in that huge house so it served its purpose well.

Louisa fell in love with a charming boy called Johnnie Ramsay. Johnnie was handsome and the toast of the town, as was Louisa. They had a lot in common as he loved the country and was a good shot. Henry and I organised the wedding and on a fine summer morning on 25th July 1981 we all walked down to the little West Wratting Church, which was just at the bottom of the field. Louisa was dressed in white muslin and looked like a lovely swan, carrying masses of orange blossom. The reception was at the house, which looked beautiful decorated with flowers, and a marquee on the lawn. Henry walked his sister down the aisle, but I missed Erland very much and felt sad that he couldn't see the daughter he loved so well, and the house at its best, all dressed up for a wedding. Louisa beamed all day.

They went to India for their honeymoon and we all felt sad as she was the first child to leave the home. Johnnie was utterly charming. Luckily Louisa and Johnnie were entrepreneurial and started up a shop in Chelsea, buying pretty prints cheaply and framing them well. She and Johnnie ran the business together successfully. Their son Christopher was born on 19th February 1984 and their daughter Lucy Emma in 1985. My first grandchild was a totally endearing little chap. Very inquisitive, he couldn't be left for a second at any age. His great treat was to play golf. Christopher did well at Eton and then embarked on an extraordinary gap year, when he was always ringing up for either help or money from a back-of-beyond country. No grandmother could wish for a sweeter little girl than Lucy. She was very popular with the whole family and loved all the family traditions, Belvoir for Christmas, festivities at Haddon and weekends at West Wratting.

After years of gallivanting Henry married in 1989 at the age of thirty-four. His beautiful bride was Tatjana Schoeller, the daughter of Austrian-born socialite Eva O'Neill. Tatjana was half German and half Austrian and had had an international education. They married at a registry office in London. I think it's sad to do it that way, but two weeks later they married at a big church in Paris which was followed by a dinner at the Ritz. Louisa and I flew to Paris together and stayed at the Hotel Bristol. Tatjana looked very pretty in a perfectly straight silk sheath dress with a circlet of mixed flowers in her hair. Harry Somerset was the Best Man. It was all foreign to me but I loved the Ritz and particularly enjoyed the singing of Eva's American husband. If you closed your eyes it could have been Frank Sinatra singing.

The old saying that a daughter is a daughter for all your life but a son's a son until he has a wife is very true. I can understand it because I had found it difficult to get along with my mother-in-law, Erland's stepmother. His real mother died young and his father married again a very tough woman who was in a different world to me. She wouldn't give us any help when we were struggling at West Wratting in the early days. She had one daughter herself, and when she died she left all the grandchildren some money each, but there wasn't much to leave as she was a jolly good spender.

Henry had inherited West Wratting equally with Louisa and Richard but bought them out in 1983. He and Tatjana now live there with their three delightful children: Anouska born in 1991, Celina, 1996 and Jasper, 2001. Apart from being a fine singer, the eldest Anouska is intelligent and now studying at Duke University in America. Celina looks so much like her mother while Jasper is a carbon copy of Henry as a child and is adorable, which is wonderful for their grandmother. They entertain continually at West Wratting because Henry has made the shoot very good. They have done away with all the cattle and I miss the cows grazing in front of the house. Now it's all arable with a break crop of sugar beet.

The mid-18th century house retains its original mouldings and the late 18th century wing has a dining room and a drawing room rising the full height. These two larger rooms lend themselves to entertaining. The house has the blessing of both worlds as you can use the grand rooms when you want while in the older part there is a kitchen and smaller dining room of equal beauty. As Henry is also an entrepreneur the house is generally full of business people and those who like shooting.

They use all the rooms, even the little flat above the stables. Guests come by helicopter from all over the world. They ski and go to Florida and Henry plays golf and travels internationally. Henry's office, with a secretary he has had for years, is based at the farm and they have bought a second house in London.

My younger son Richard wanted to go for a holiday to America. I sent him off with my blessing; he ended up getting married to an older woman and settling there. He eventually divorced and now works for a large successful firm and is doing very well, but I miss him desperately.

In 1999 I decided to sell Kensington Square. I had to find somewhere to live and Henry offered me the flat over the Orangery at West Wratting but I didn't want to be on their doorstep. I came to Notting Hill where I had originally looked at the time of renting Kensington Square, because I thought the area was more healthy up on the hills, with all the lovely big independent houses. In the 1950s I was told it was far too dangerous for a family with young children, but now it's a marvellous area. An eminent agent was showing me round and I was worried and exhausted until he showed me a place where the foyer was filled with lovely pictures. I looked at this flat and thought: 'All the furniture I like best from Kensington Square will just about fit in, even my twelve Hepplewhite chairs'.

I moved in eleven years ago and at first found it hard to settle because it was so small, but when the sun is shining it's drenched with light like a greenhouse in the afternoon. Now I have made lots of friends in the building and the day porters look after me, despite the sinking fund nearly sinking me as it increases every year. The flat is part-owned by my son Richard who lives in Los Angeles, and when he is travelling on his jaunts from Timbuktu to Iceland he stays with me, and we have such happy times. The climate on the other side of the world has beguiled him to such a degree that I don't think he will ever leave California. As you get older weather matters and dark days are not funny.

When I turned ninety Henry, Tatjana, Louisa and Dick organised a surprise birthday dinner for me at the Ritz in London. Richard had just arrived back from San Francisco and took me to what we thought was a quiet family dinner, but when we arrived to my amazement I found almost all my friends, over one hundred people altogether. I was taken aback and am sure I wasn't suitably dressed. Before we sat down to eat all the grandchildren did an act, rather like in *The Sound of Music*. Anouska sang, Celina danced and Jasper ran around with the microphone making everyone laugh. We had the most delicious foie gras with hot brioche and ended up with my favourite pudding, individual vanilla soufflés with raspberry sauce. Henry got up to make a long peroration and then we all danced to a band. All my friends broke in and danced with me but my favourite partner was Louisa's son Christopher. We danced until midnight and it was all glorious fun. Christopher is now working in the City in a firm dealing with the Far East, a job for which he was head-hunted, which is impressive in the middle of a recession. I find this very heartening and am very proud of Louisa who has been a wonderful mother.

I love to go away for the weekend with my family. Belvoir is still a lovely family home, reminiscent of my early days there. My nephew David Manners became the 11th Duke of Rutland when he succeeded to the title in 1999. He is particularly charming to me and sends me champagne with lovely letters. His wife Emma is an opera singer from Wales and is a wonder. She has five children, three girls and two boys, who love riding and are doing very well at school. She runs the castle in a way that everyone enjoys: it vibrates with the patter of little feet and is the greatest fun. It is open to the public and she is bringing back to life the gardens and the woodland which were so lovely in my childhood and had become overgrown. She runs a splendid game fair there every five years which fills the whole of the park. It is very successful and they organise it alongside the Belvoir Hunt which continues to flourish, the hounds still in their kennels.

When my brother died he left Haddon in Derbyshire to his second son, Lord Edward Manners. He enjoys it and has lovely house-parties as it is in a dream spot by the river, but it's very difficult for me now because all the floors are so undulating and the steps so steep.

Every age has its charm and although I am in my ninety-eighth year I find excitements all the time and follow the political scene worldwide as if I were in the diplomatic service. Having travelled and seen a lot I understand more than many politicians, or they would, for example, have made a better success of the Iraq war. I have friends in the City and the country, although I am a liability because I fall down like a ninepin all the time. Fortunately I haven't broken any bones.

Now I have attained this great age. Many of my dear friends are dead as door nails but I still feel ready to face a new adventure every day of my life.